I am grateful for everything! And I believe that the meaning of life is to make sense of other lives. Pedro you are the meaning of my life Love

Valene de Souza
2024

This book belong to:

____

Test Color Page

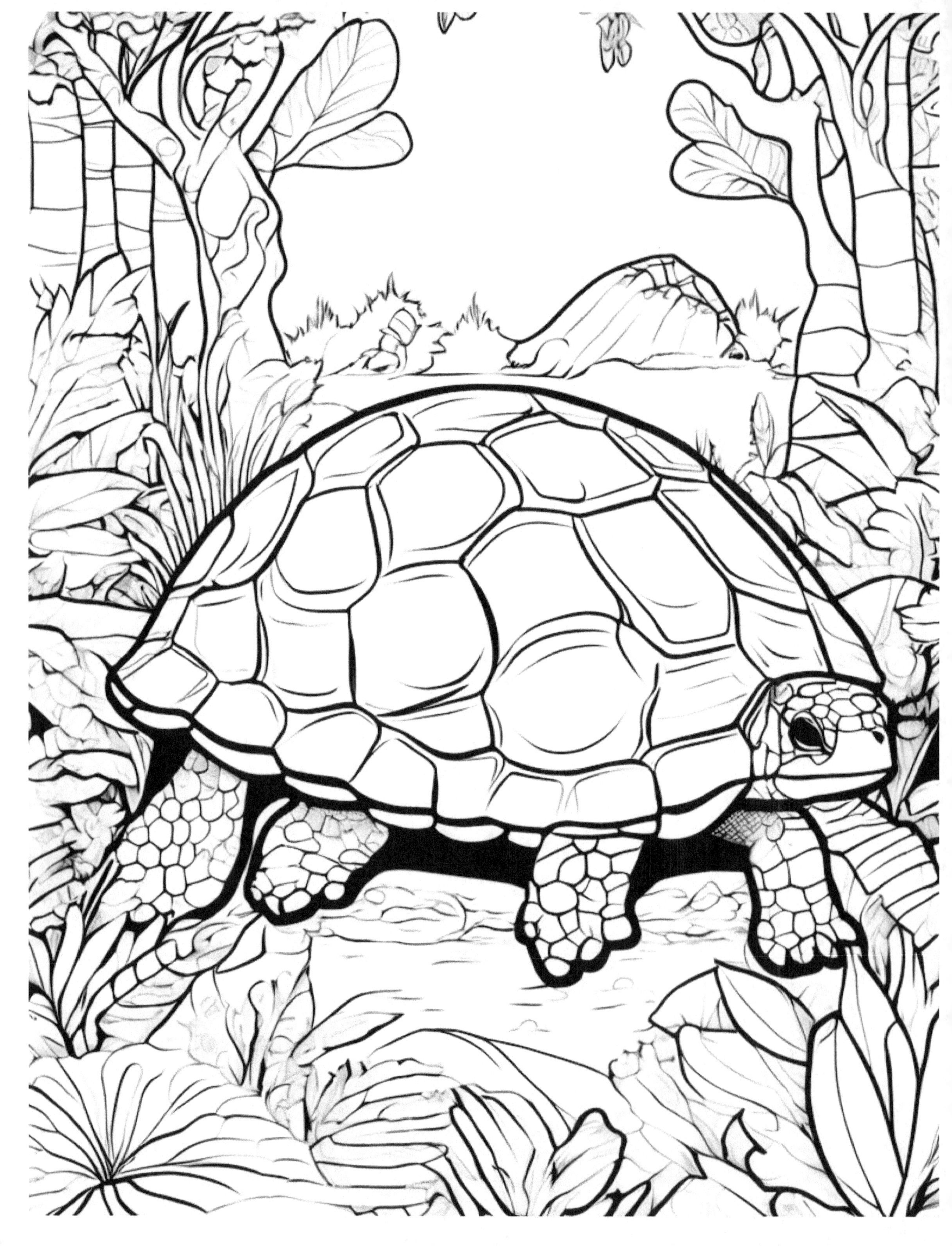

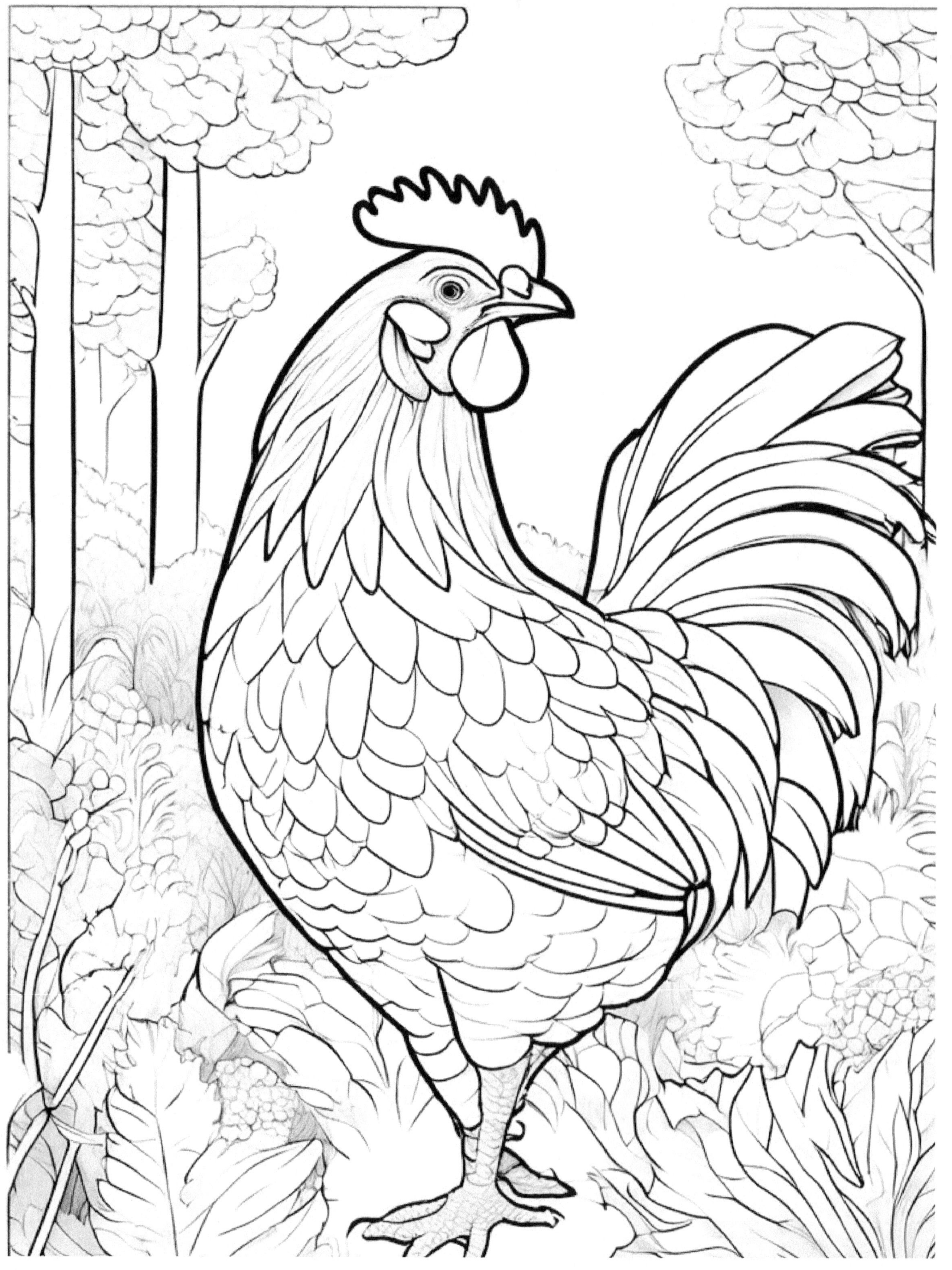

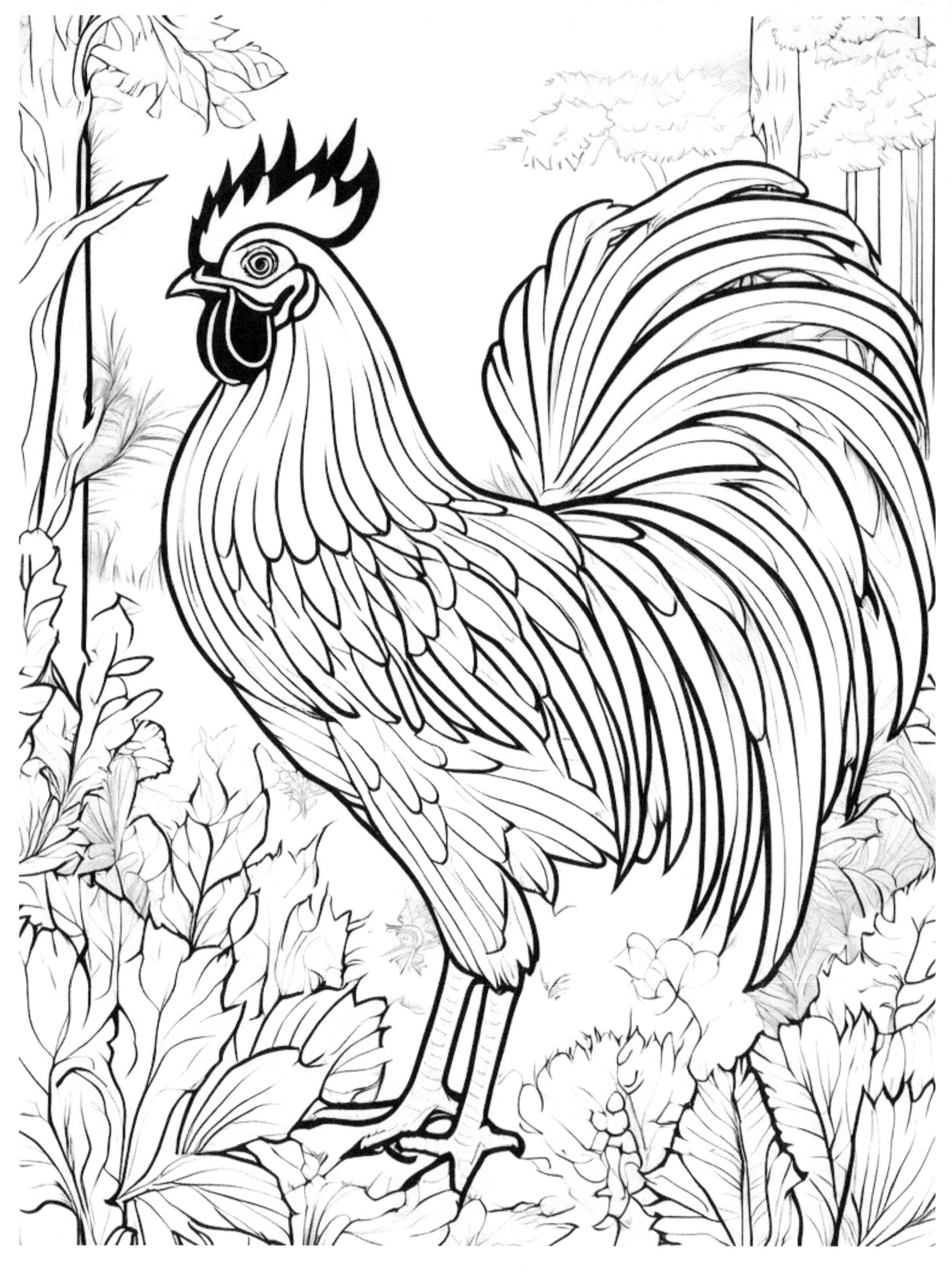

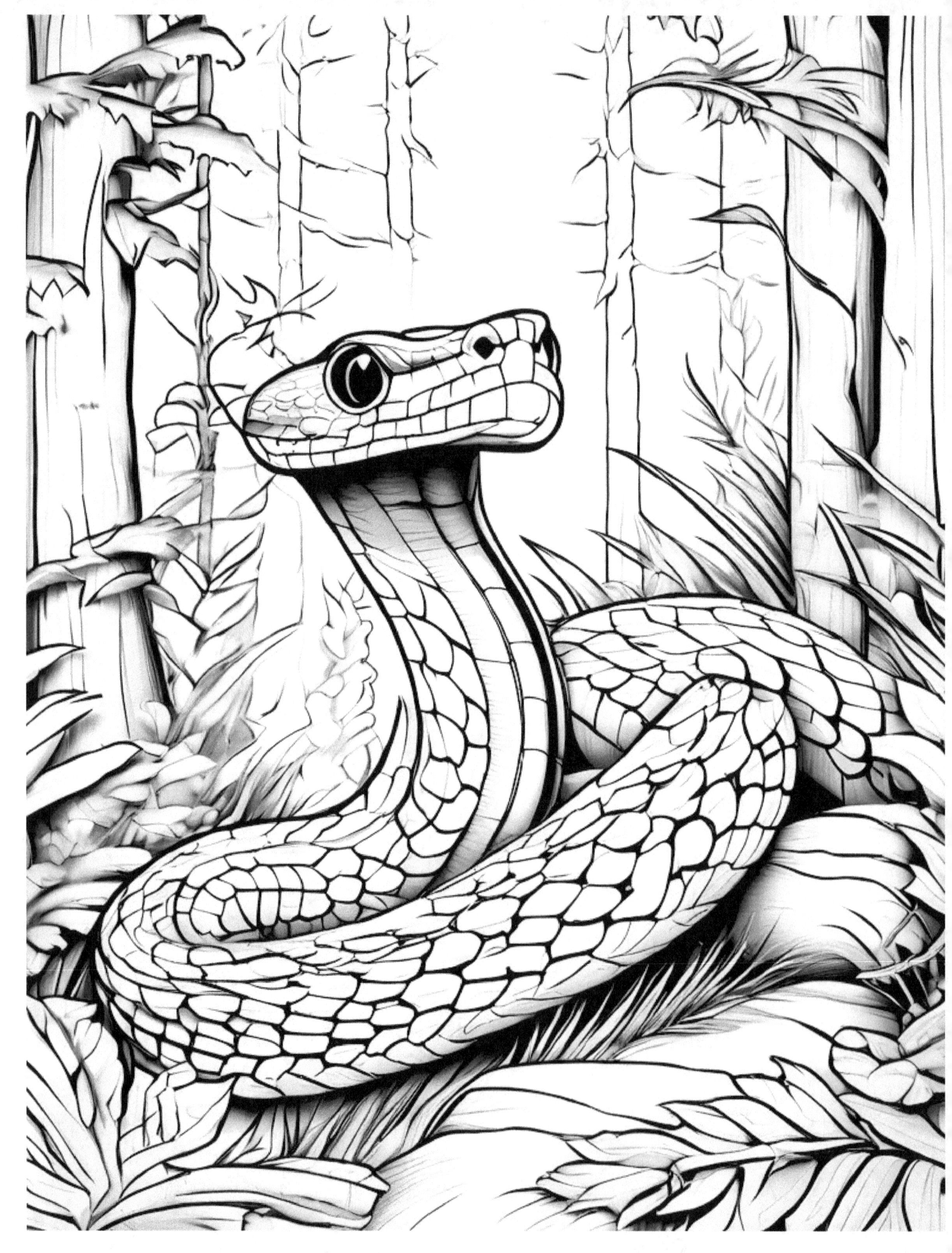

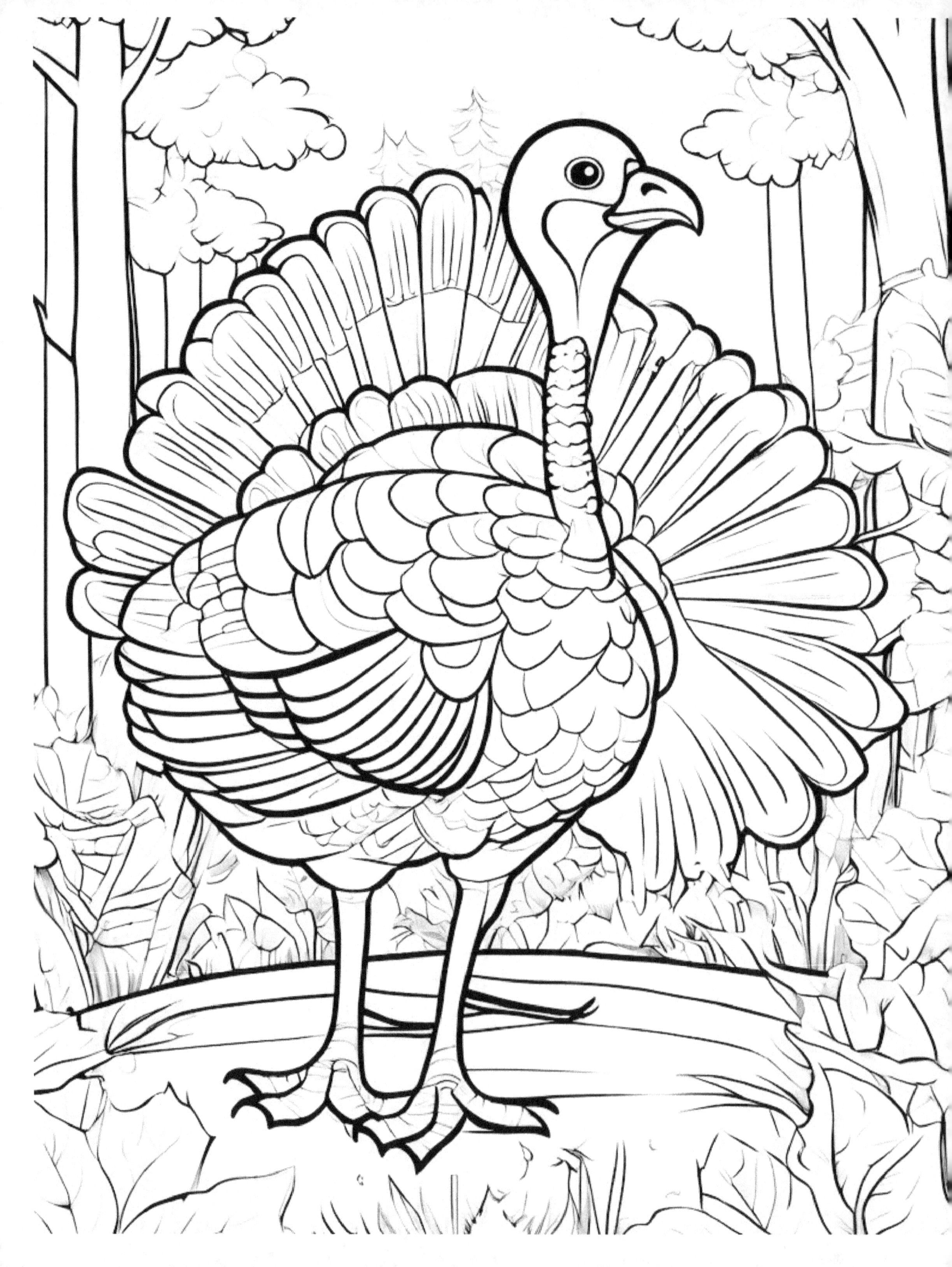

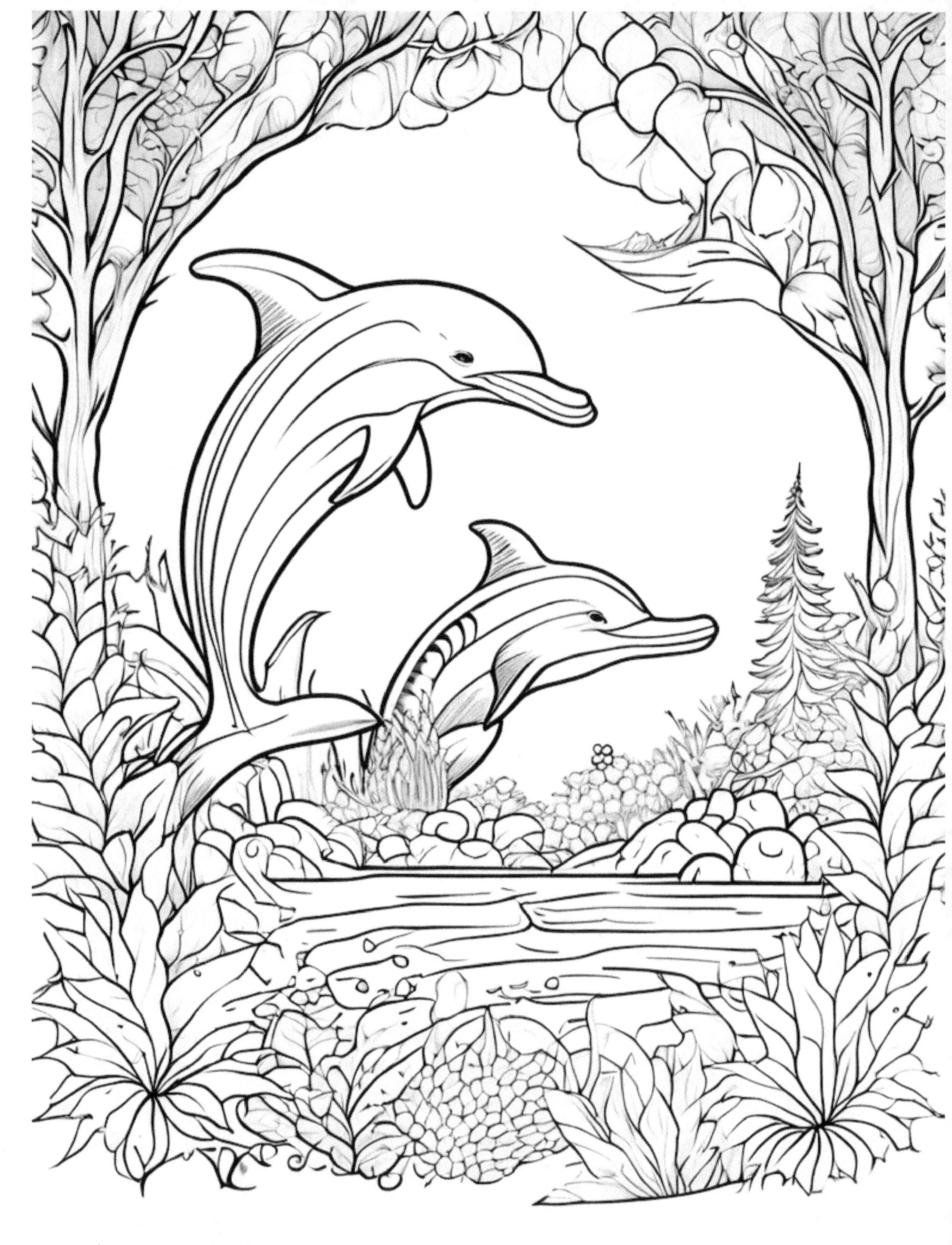

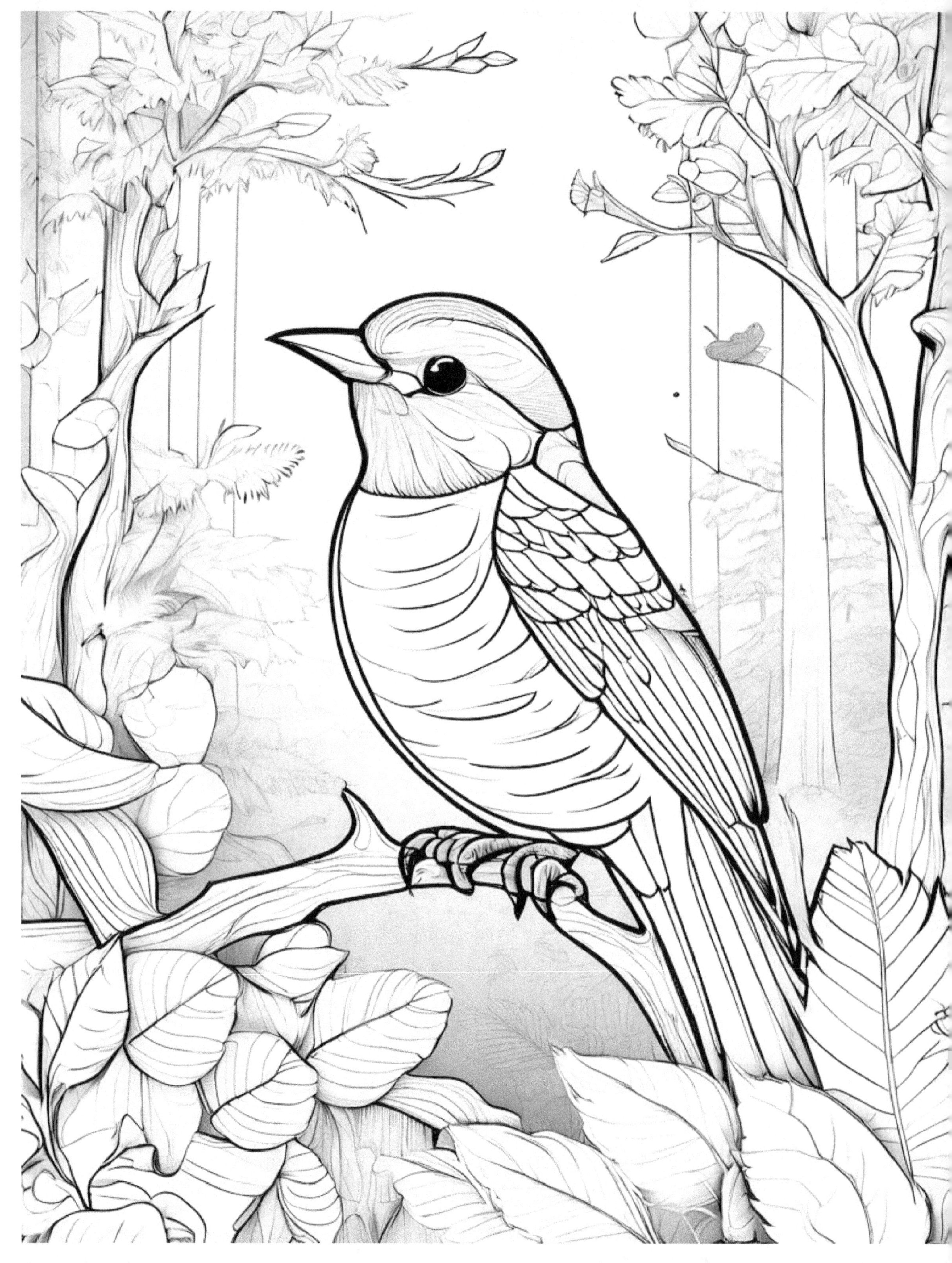

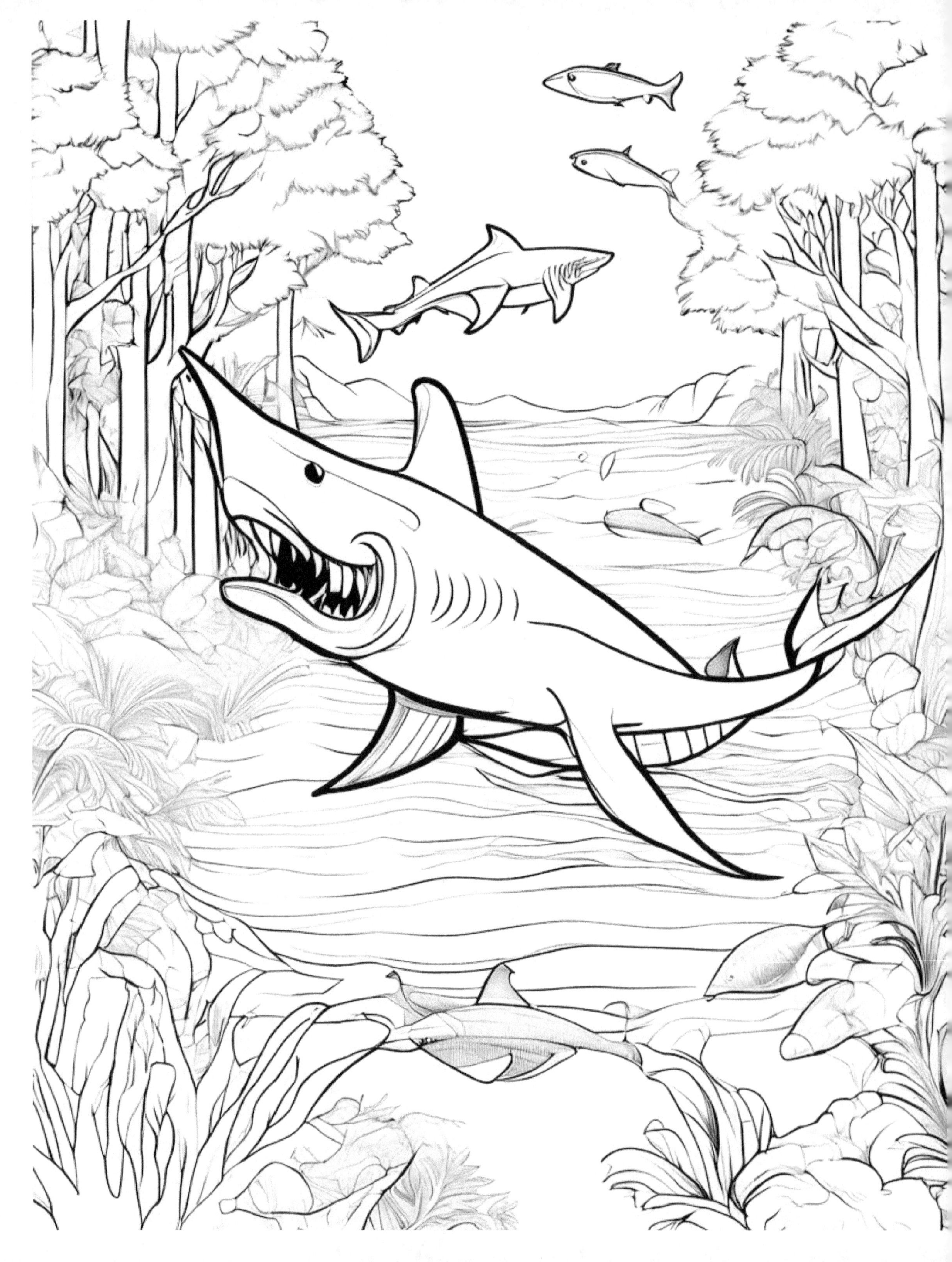

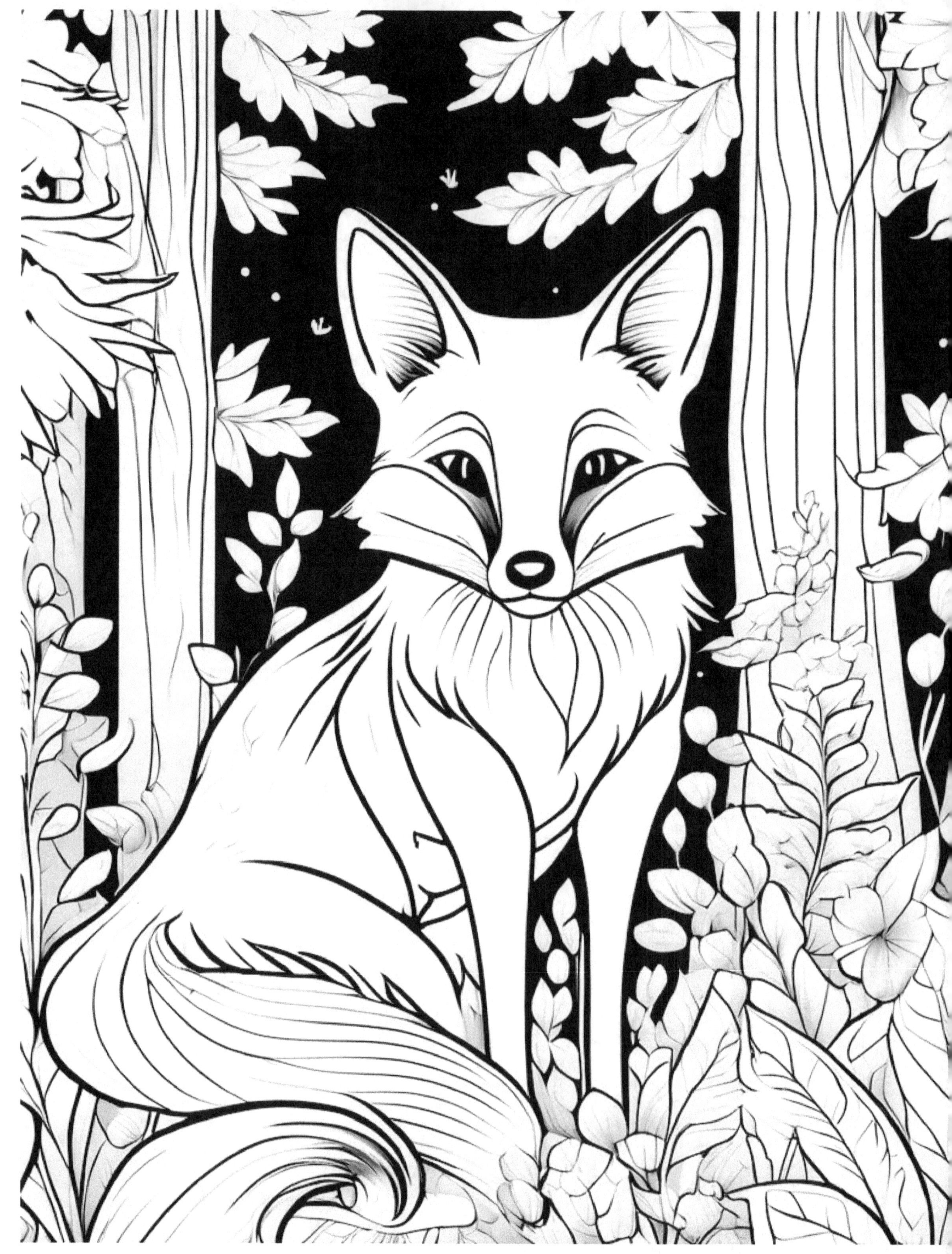

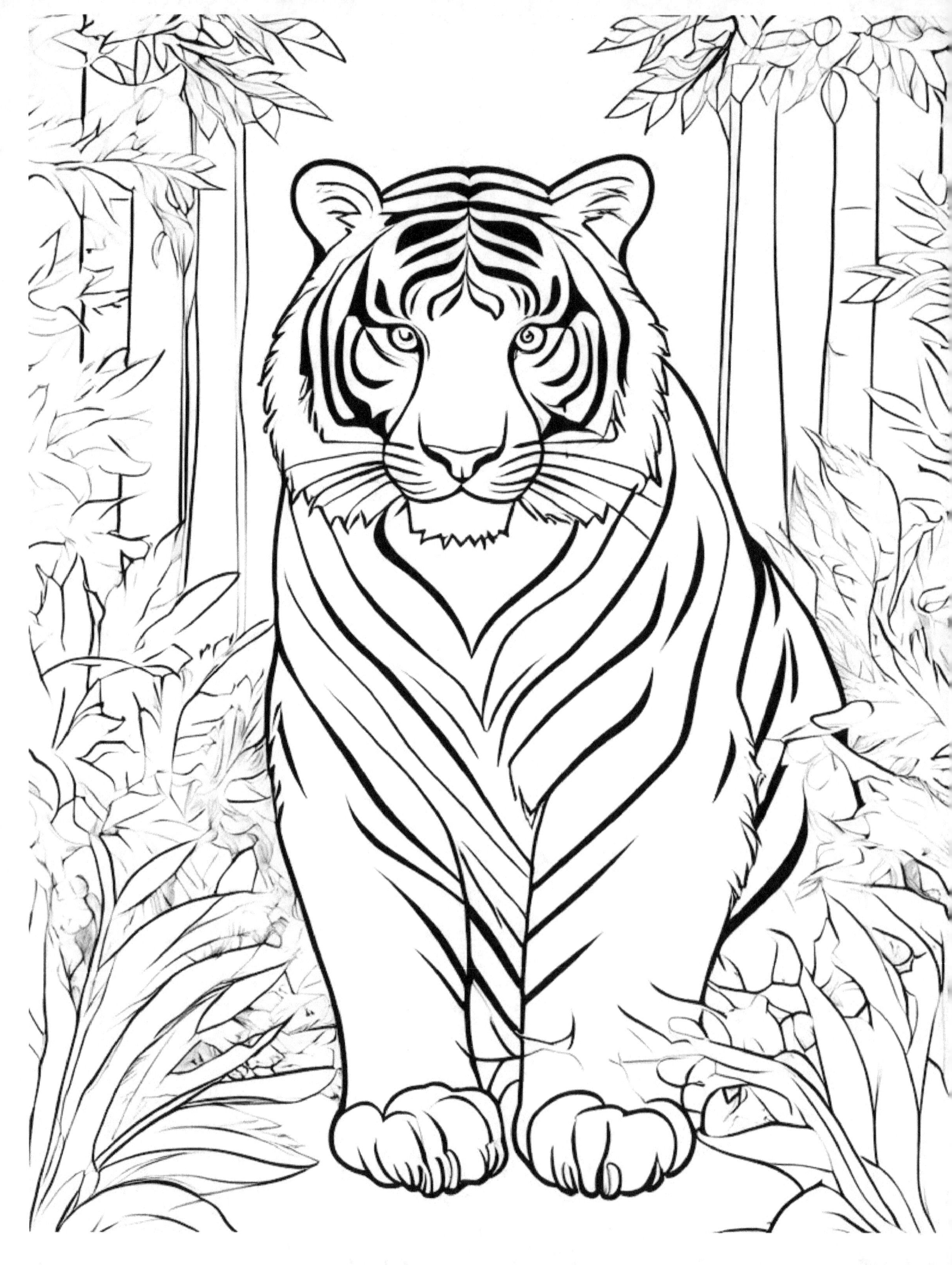

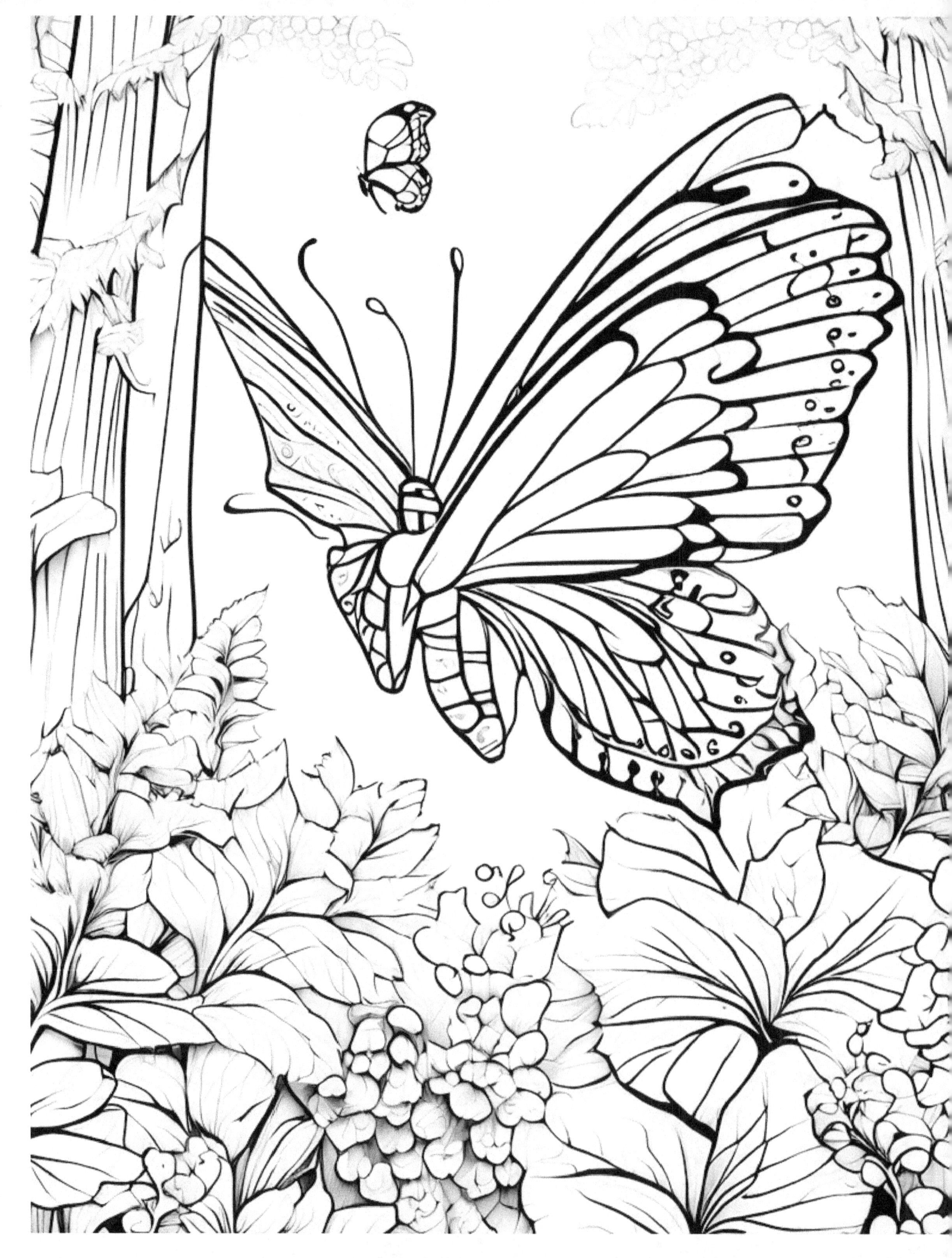

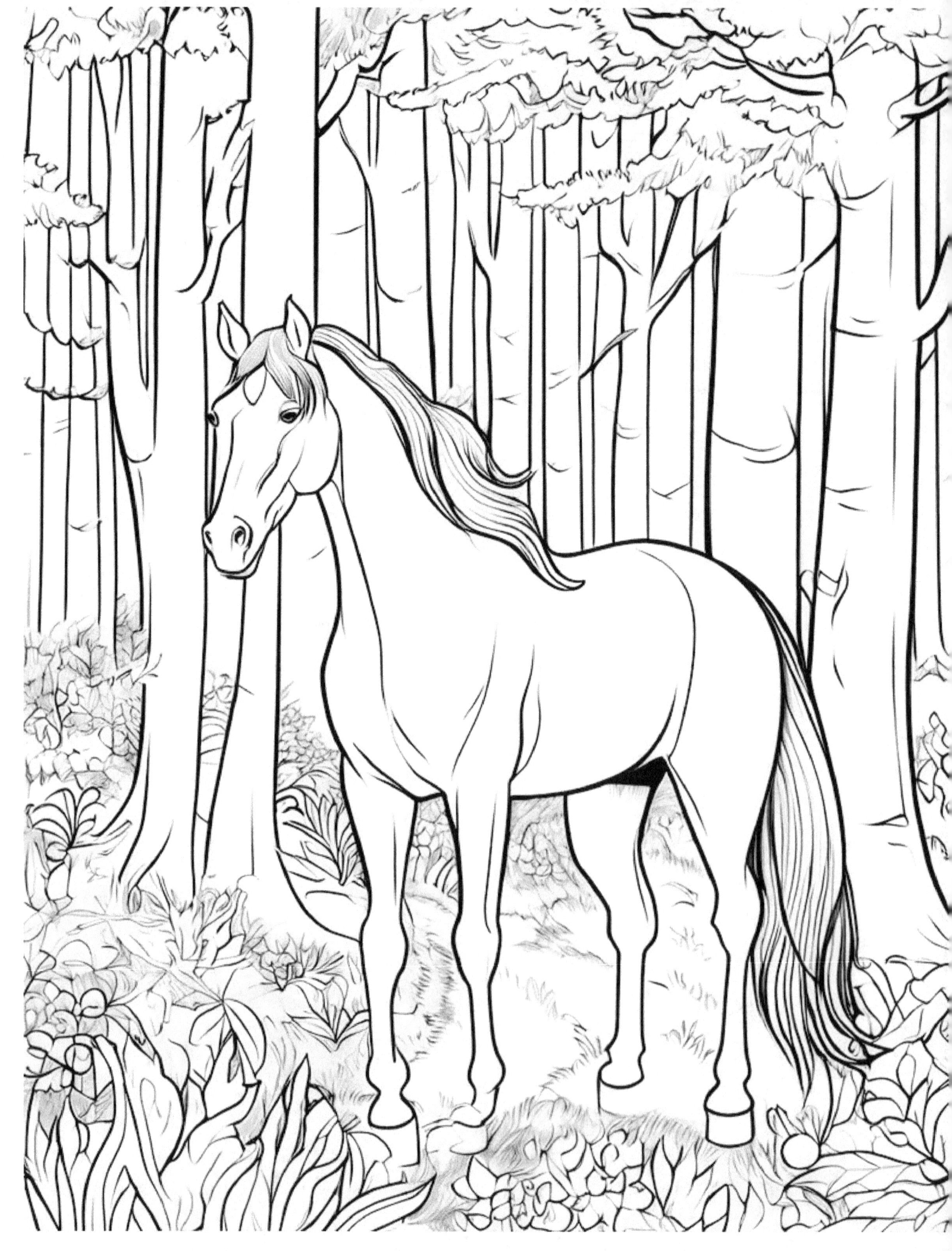

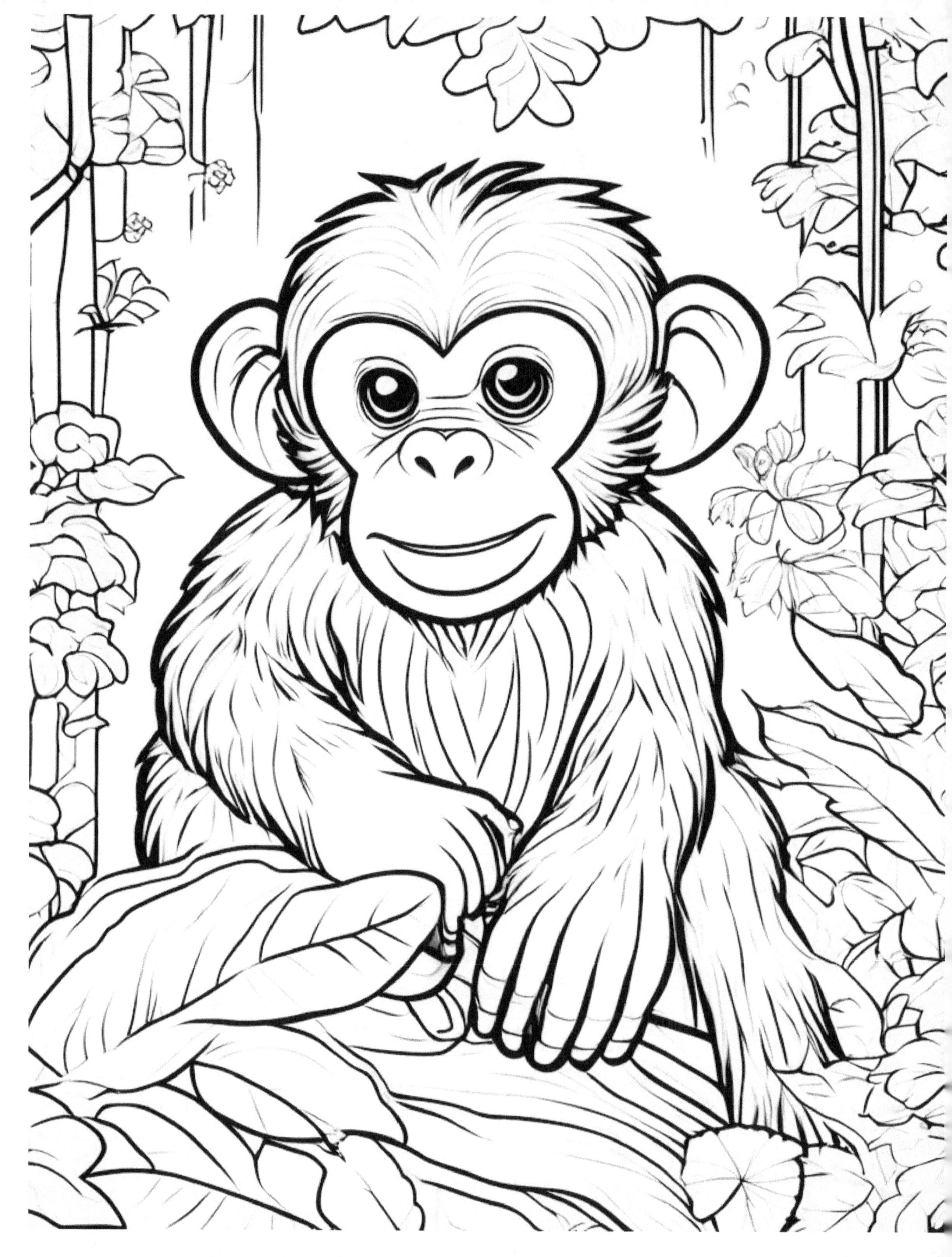

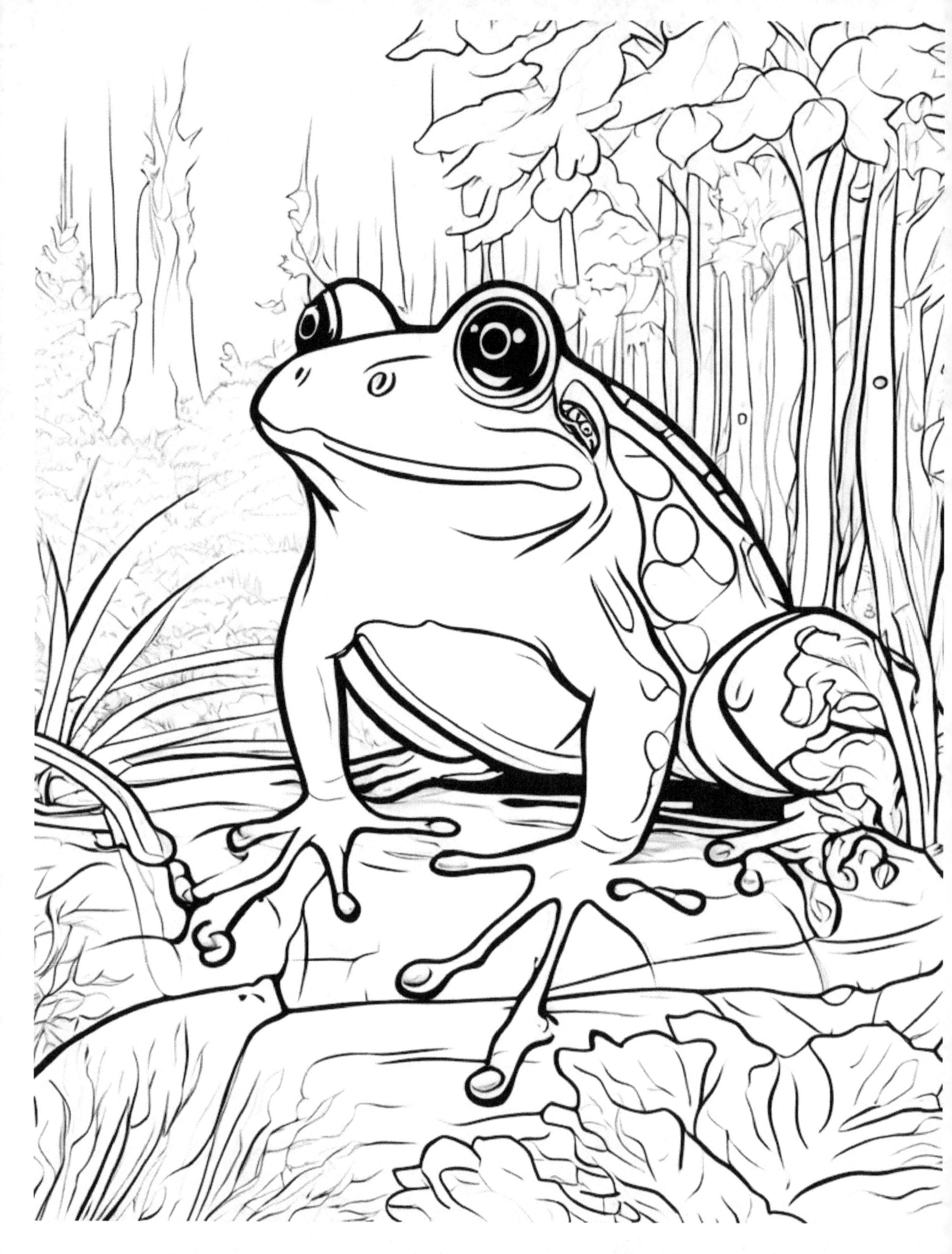

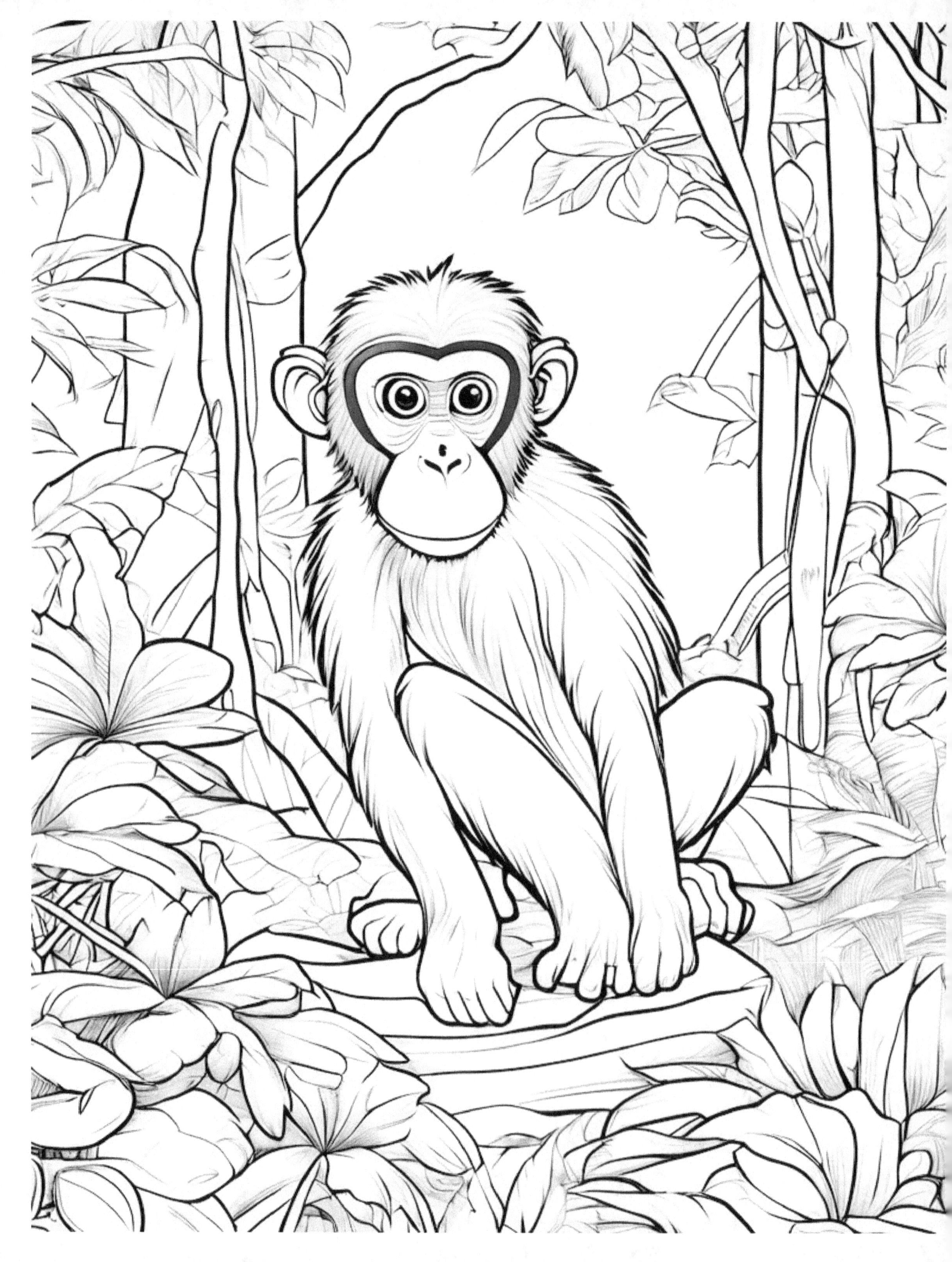

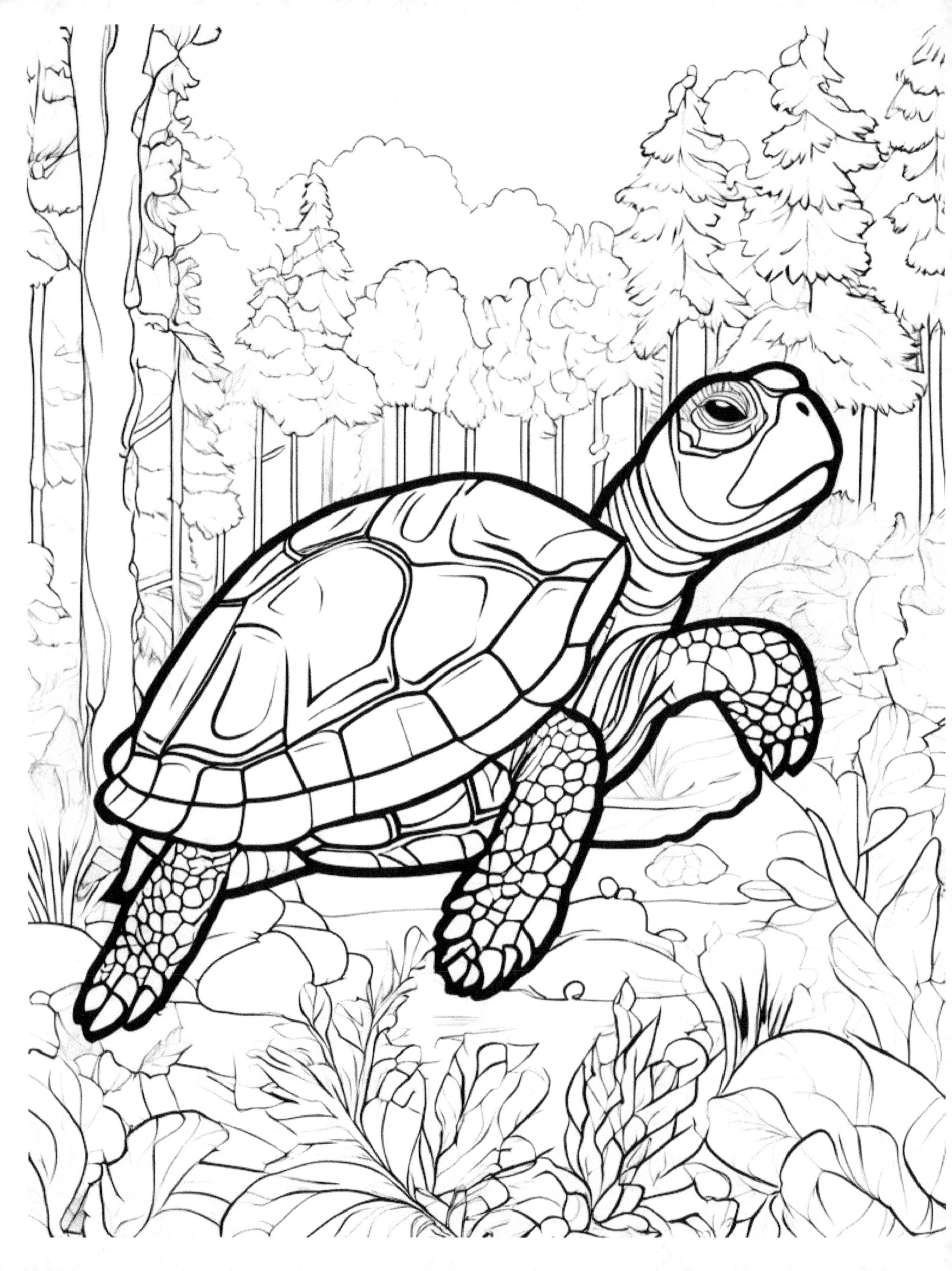

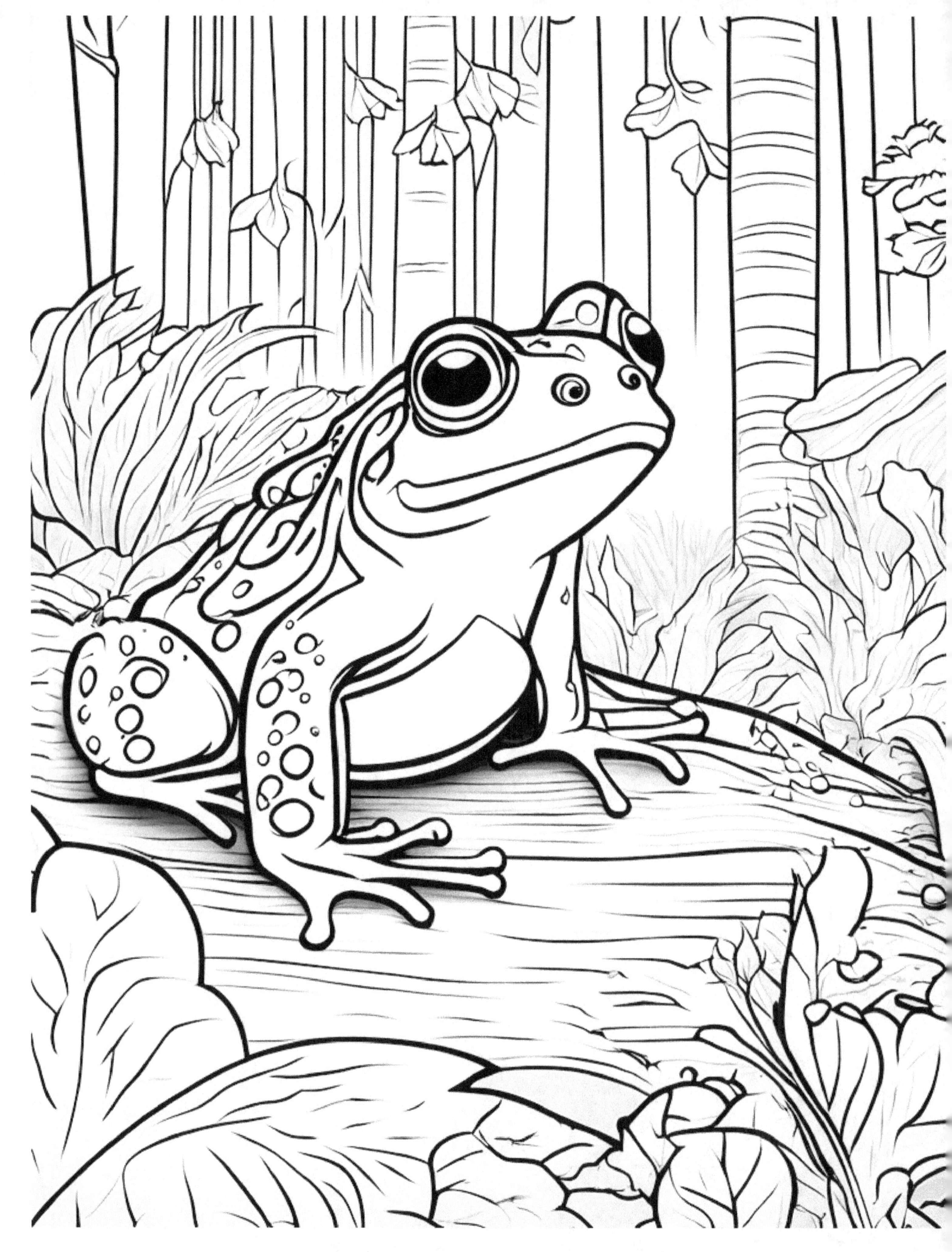

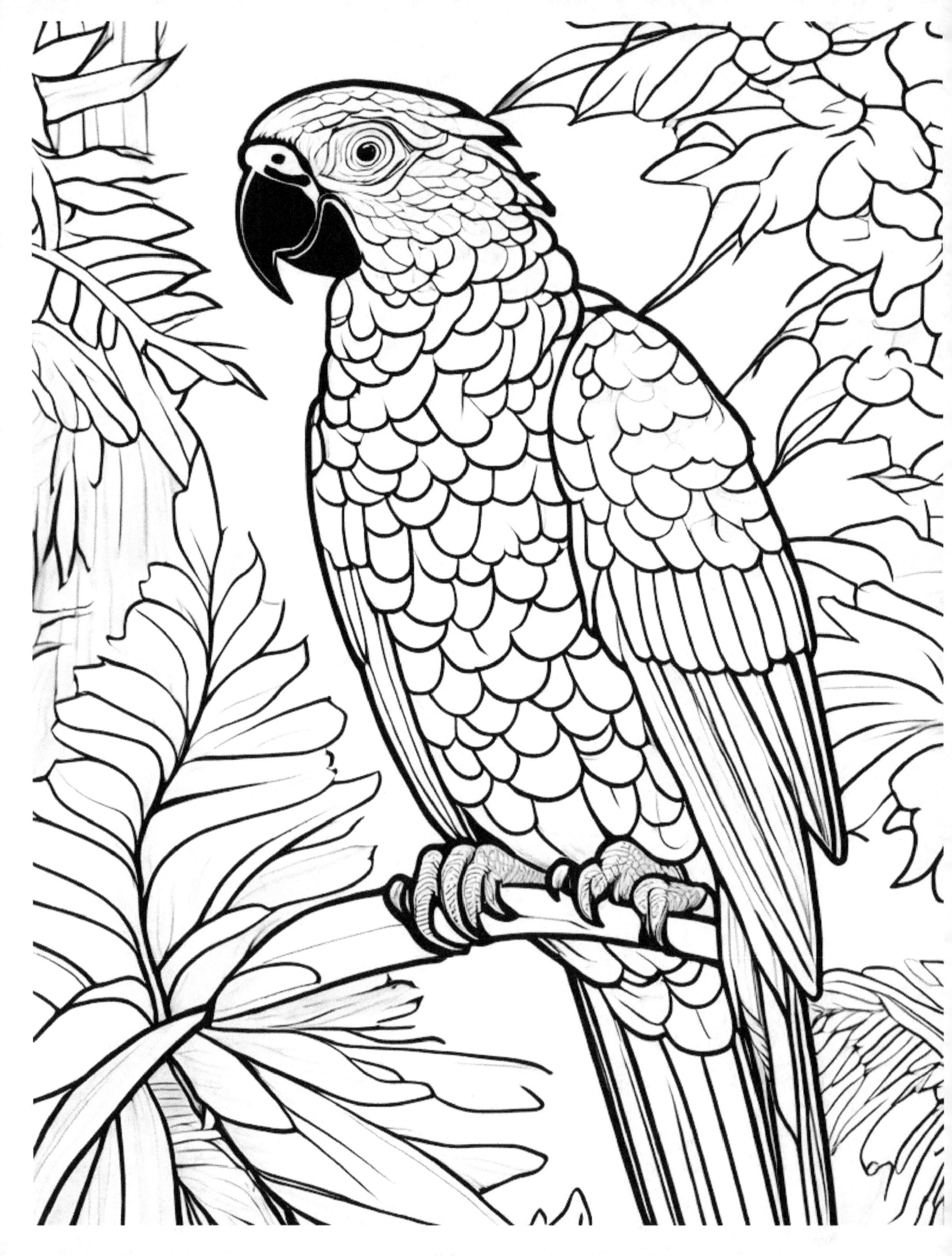

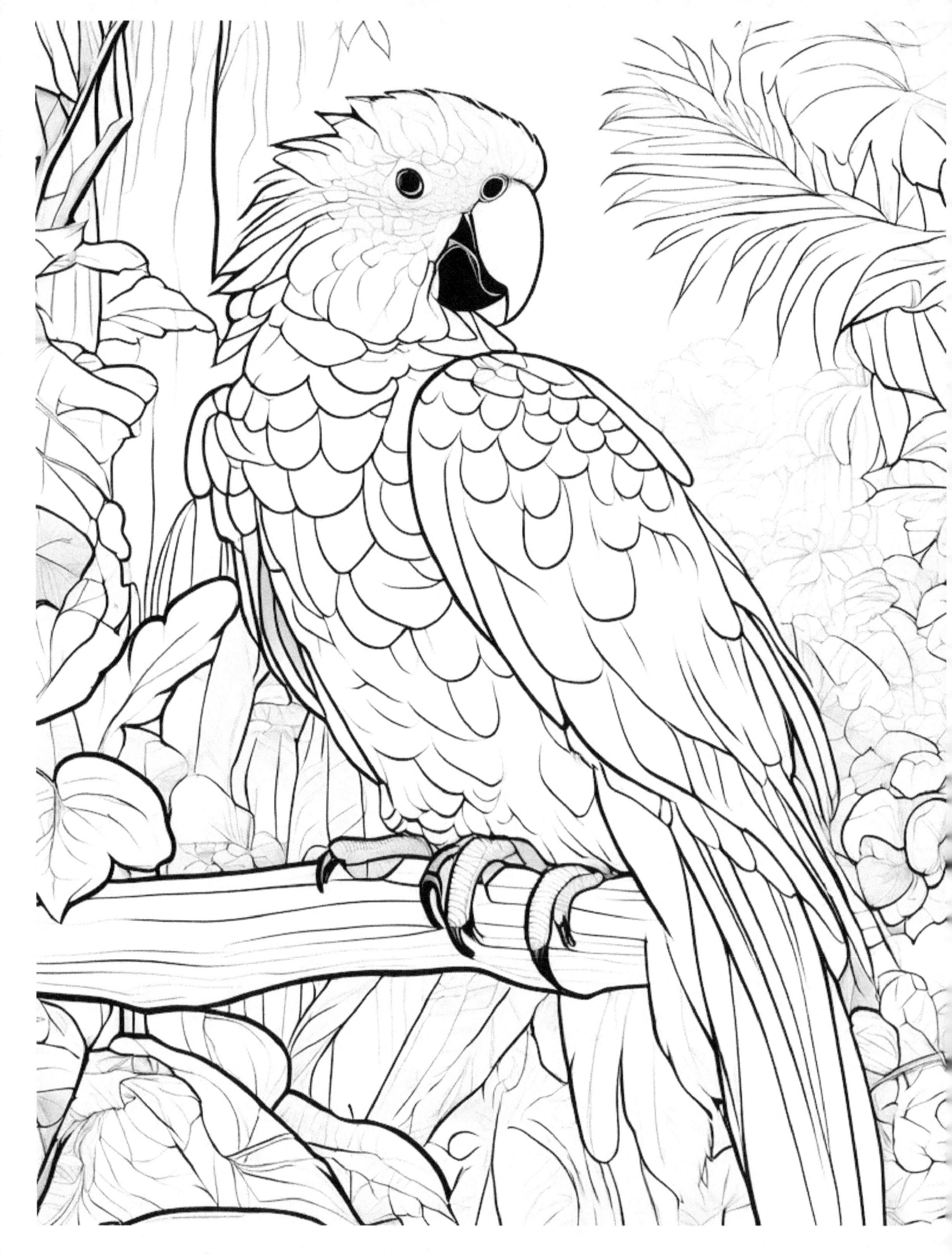

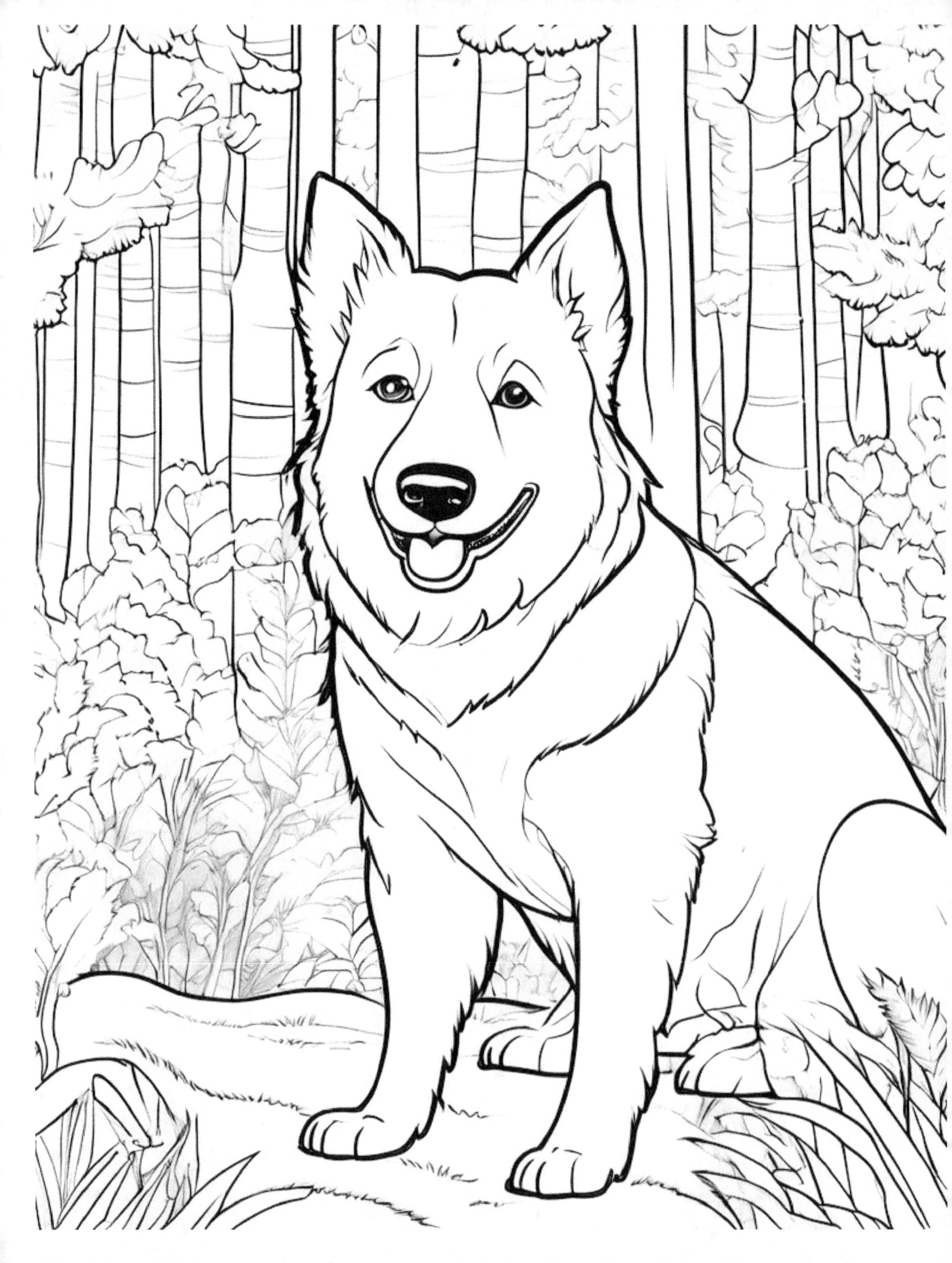

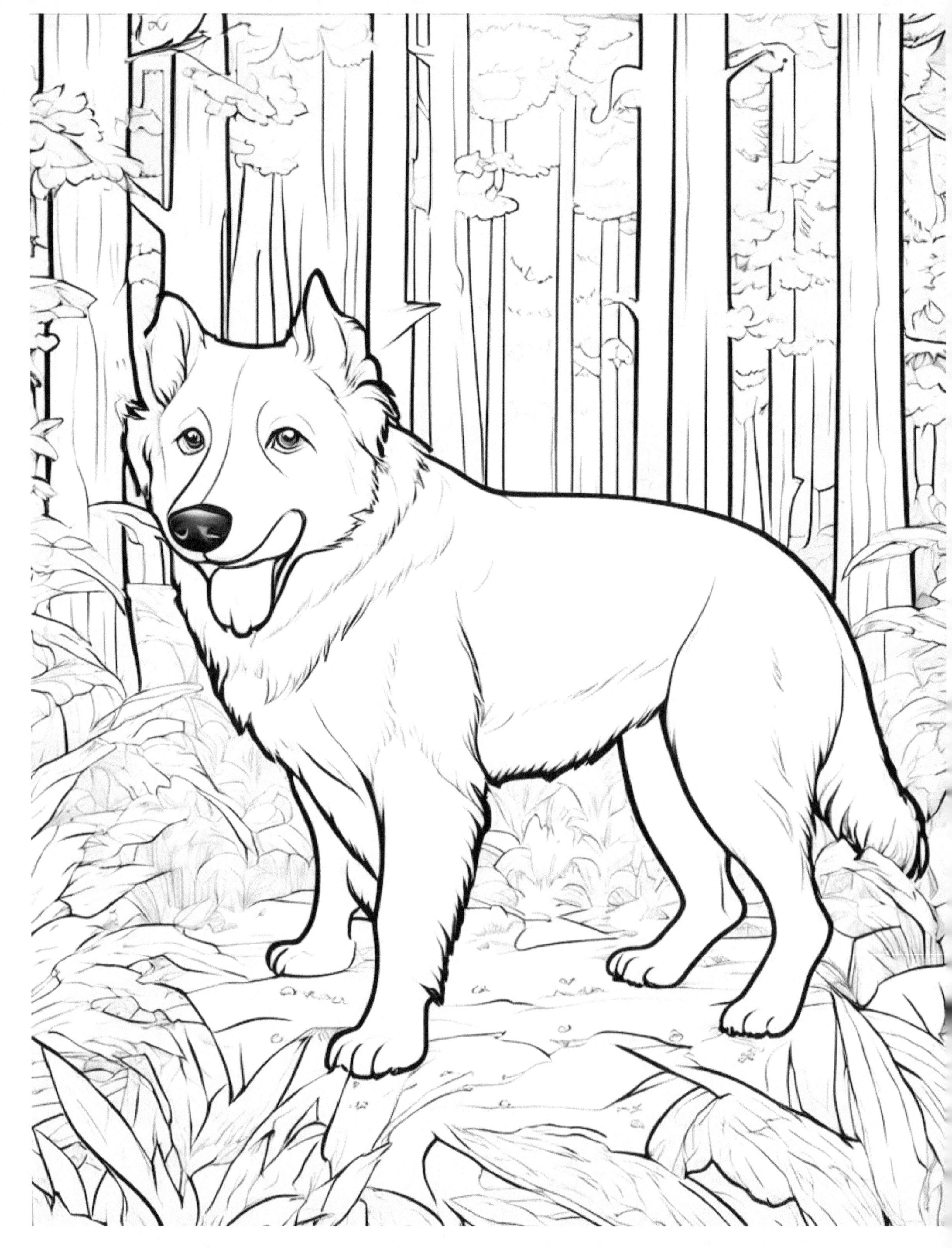

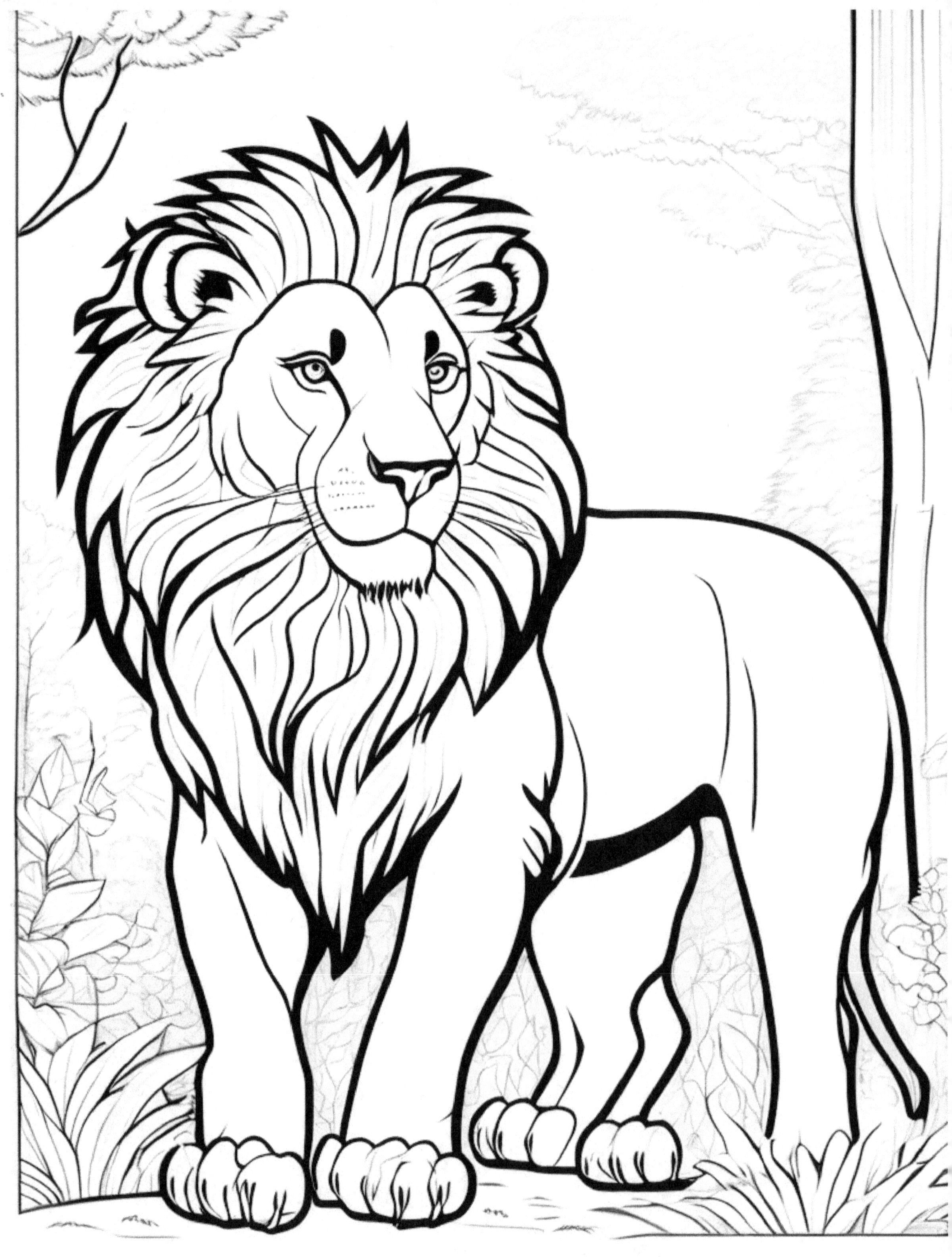

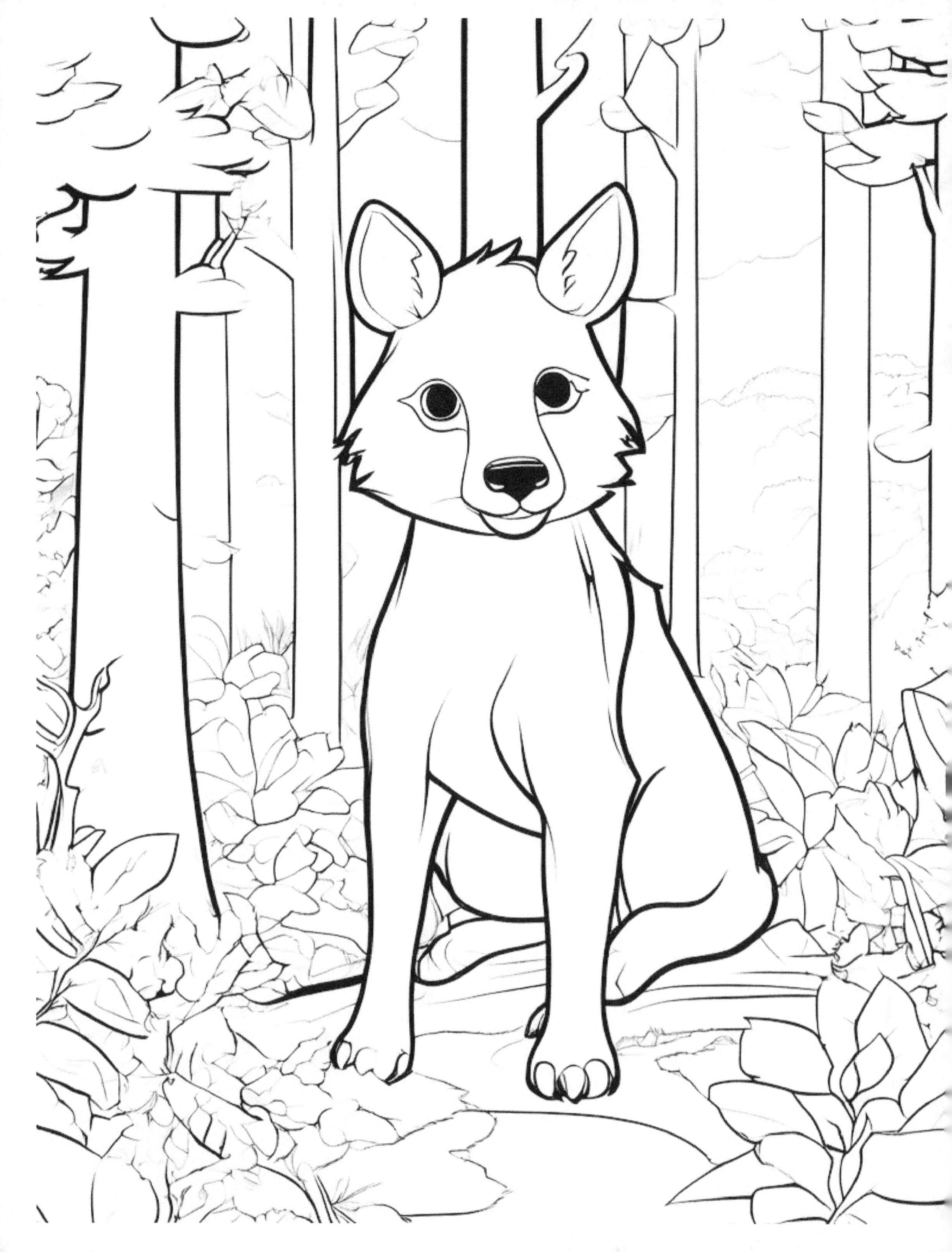

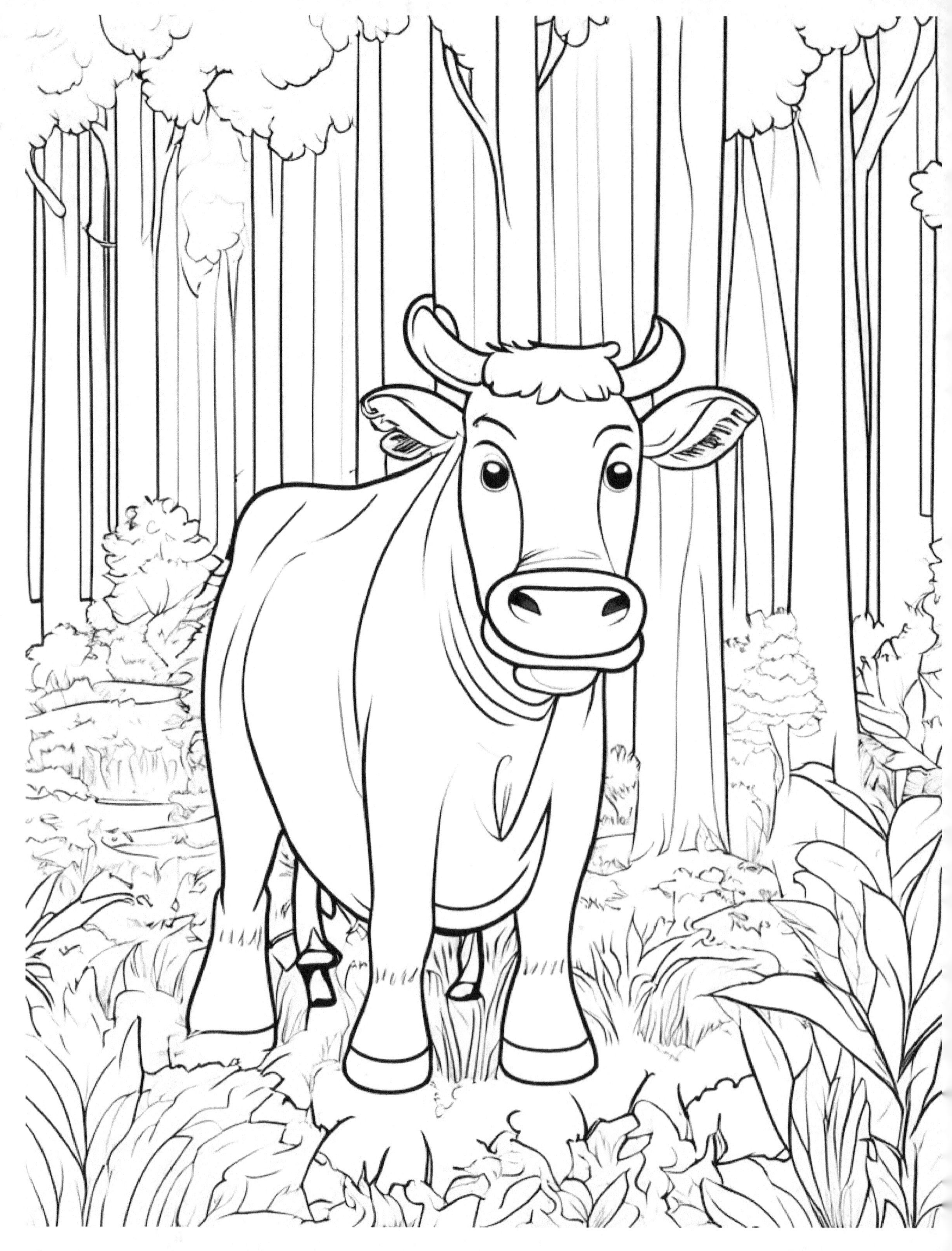

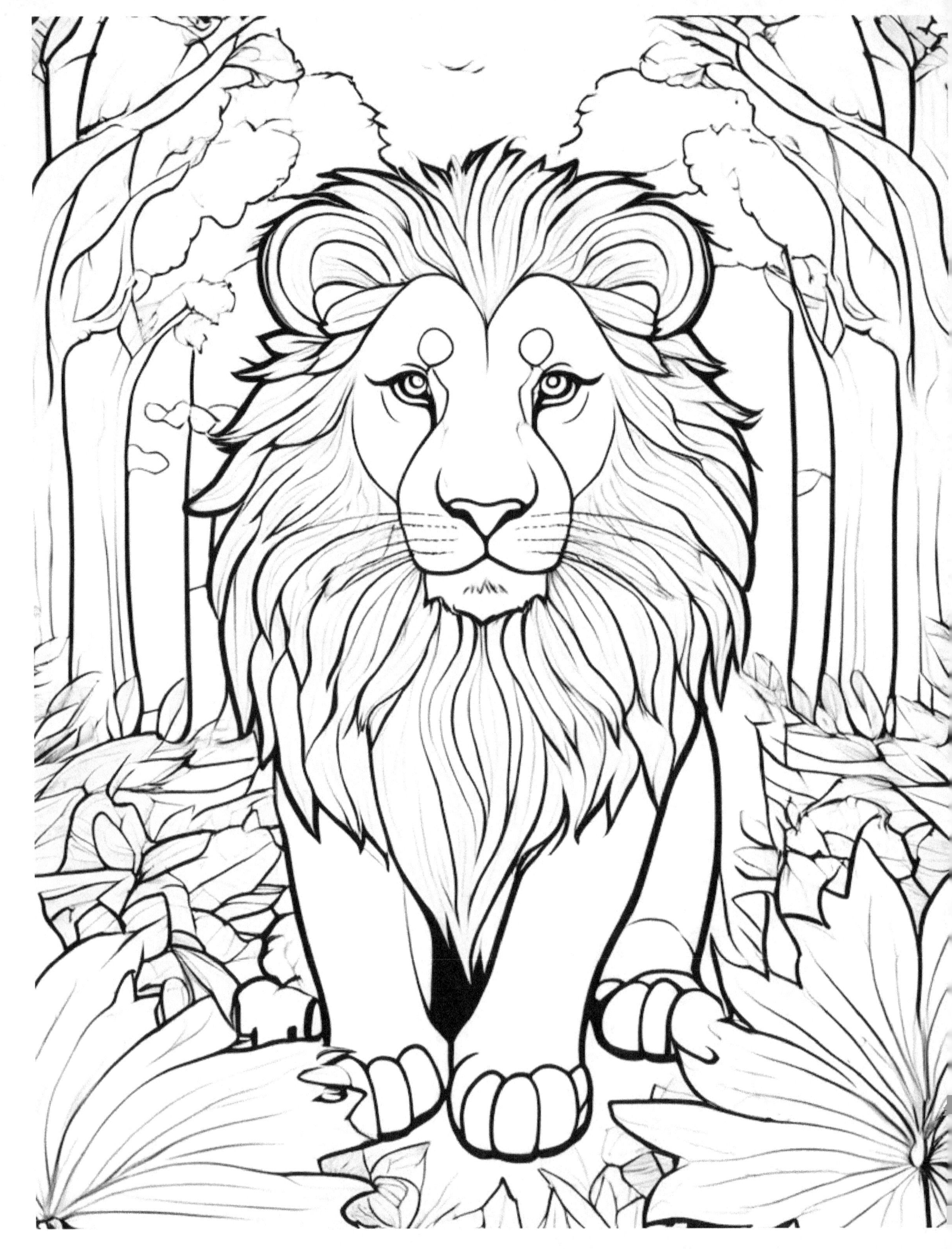

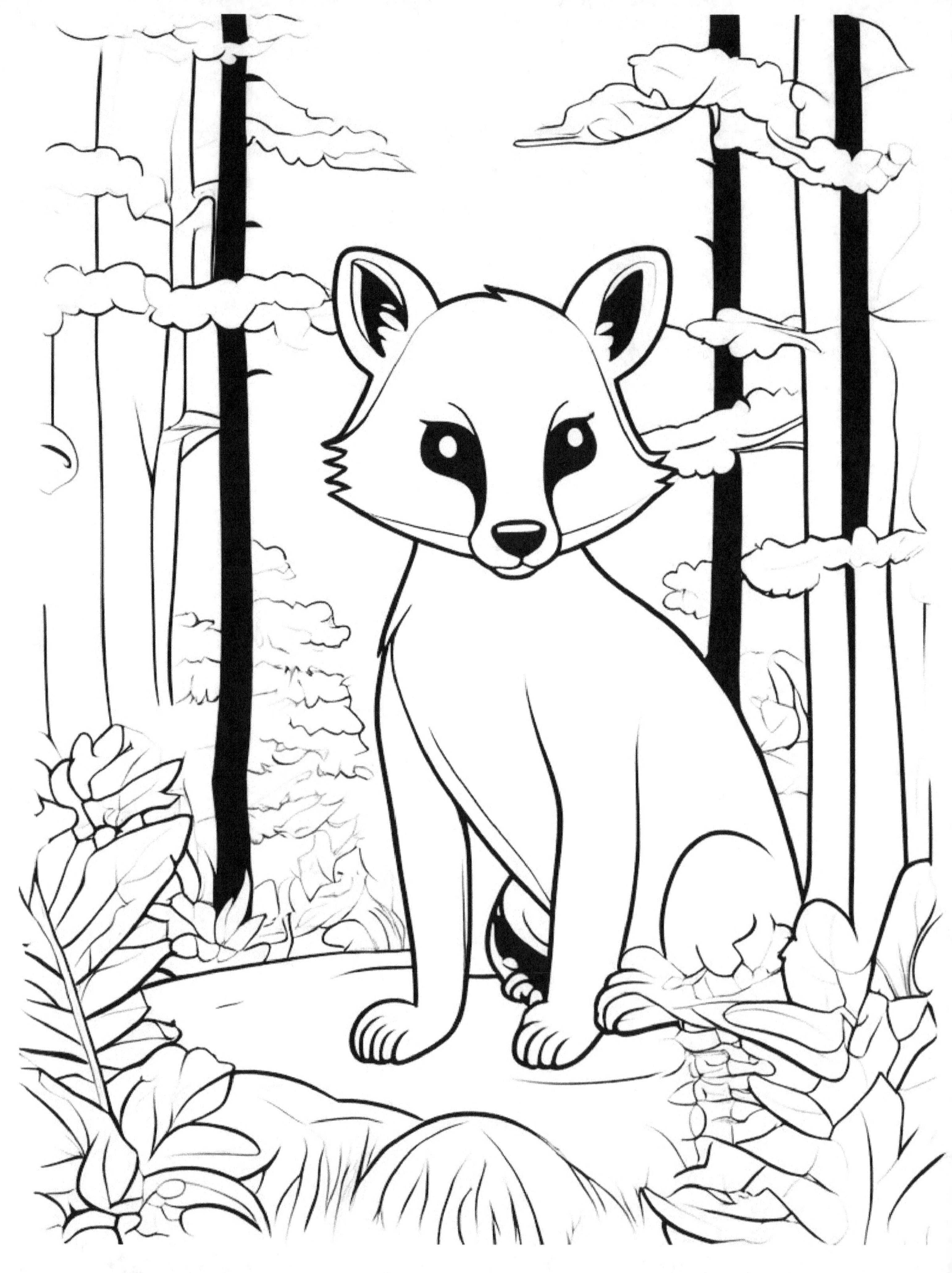

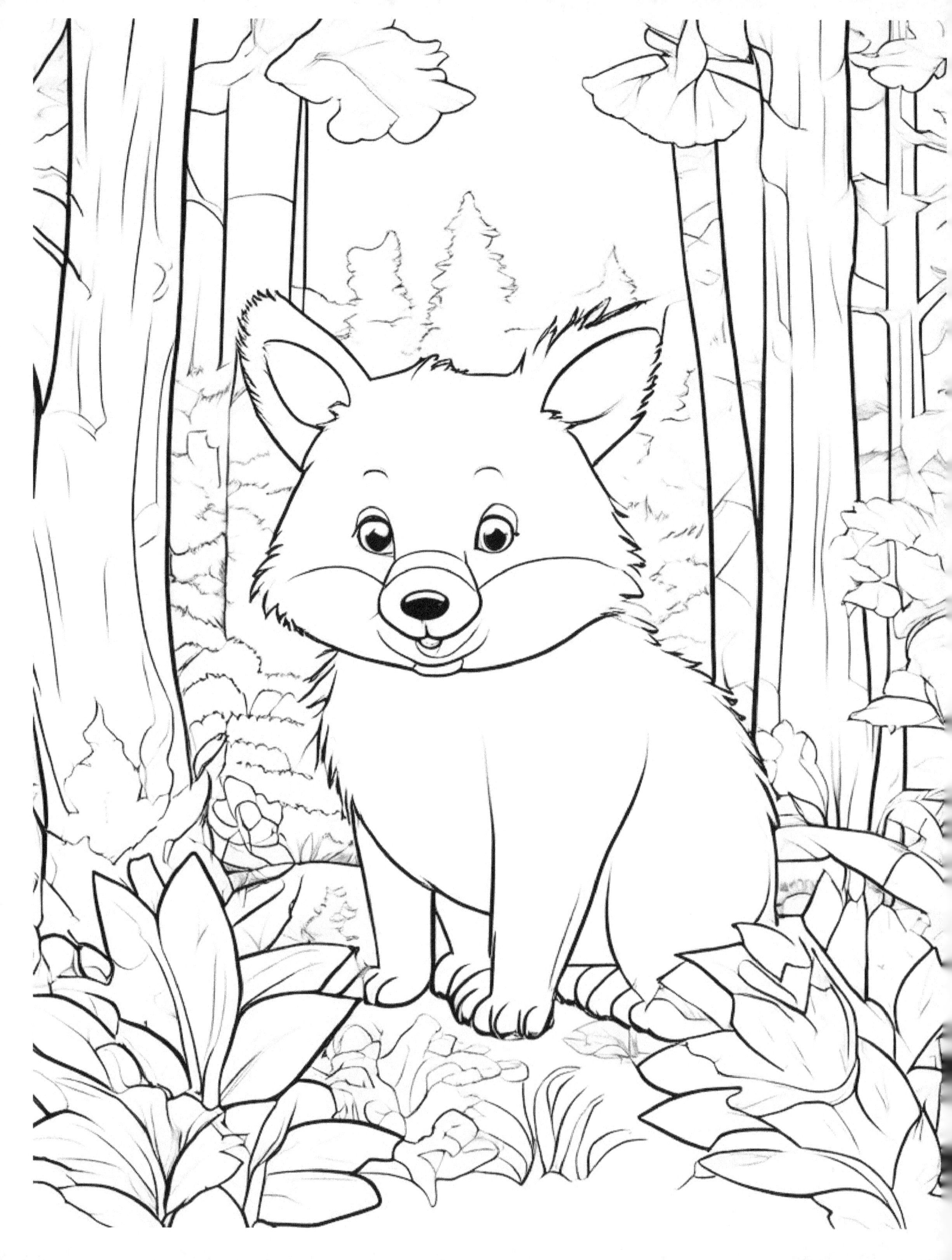

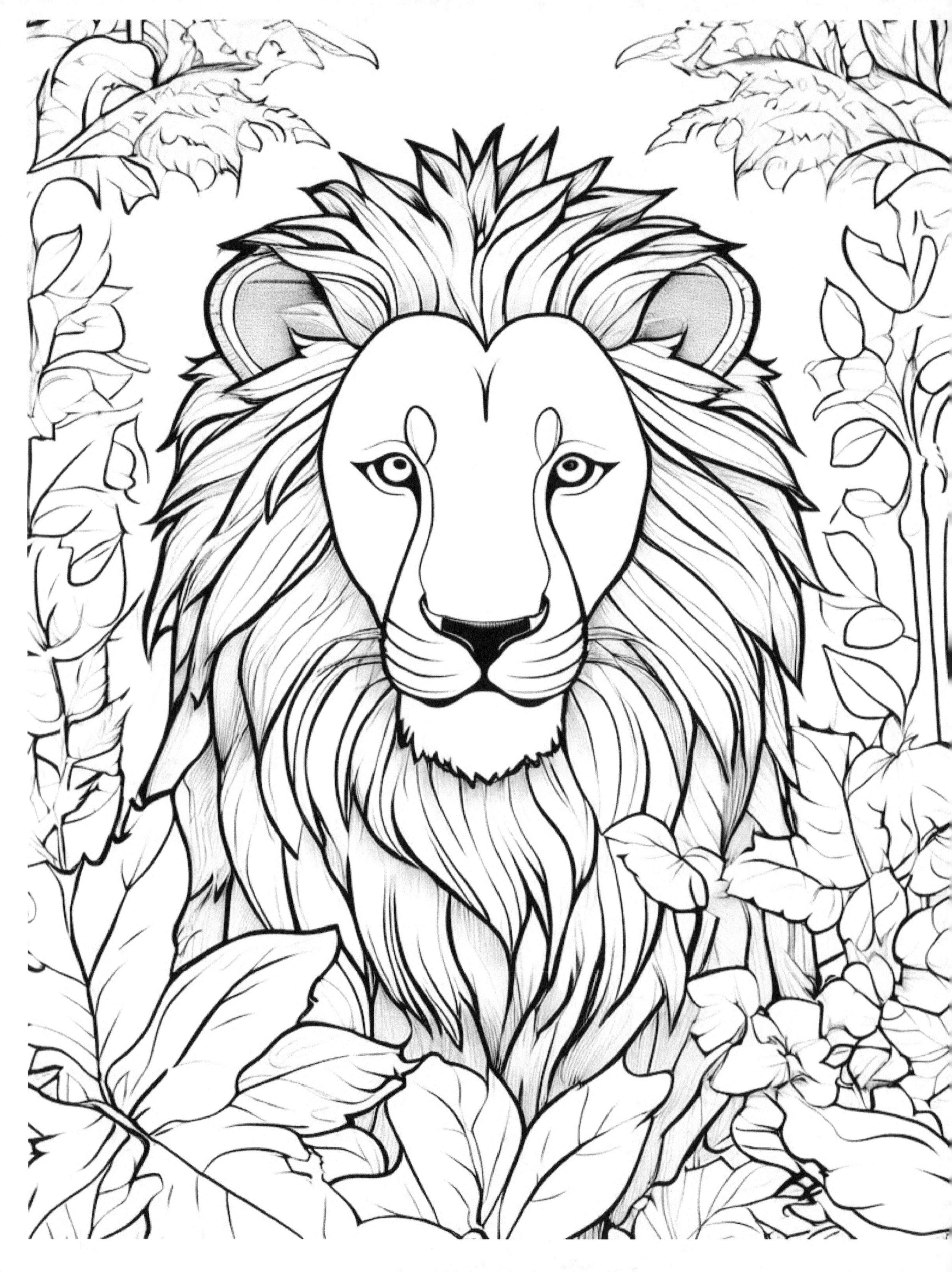

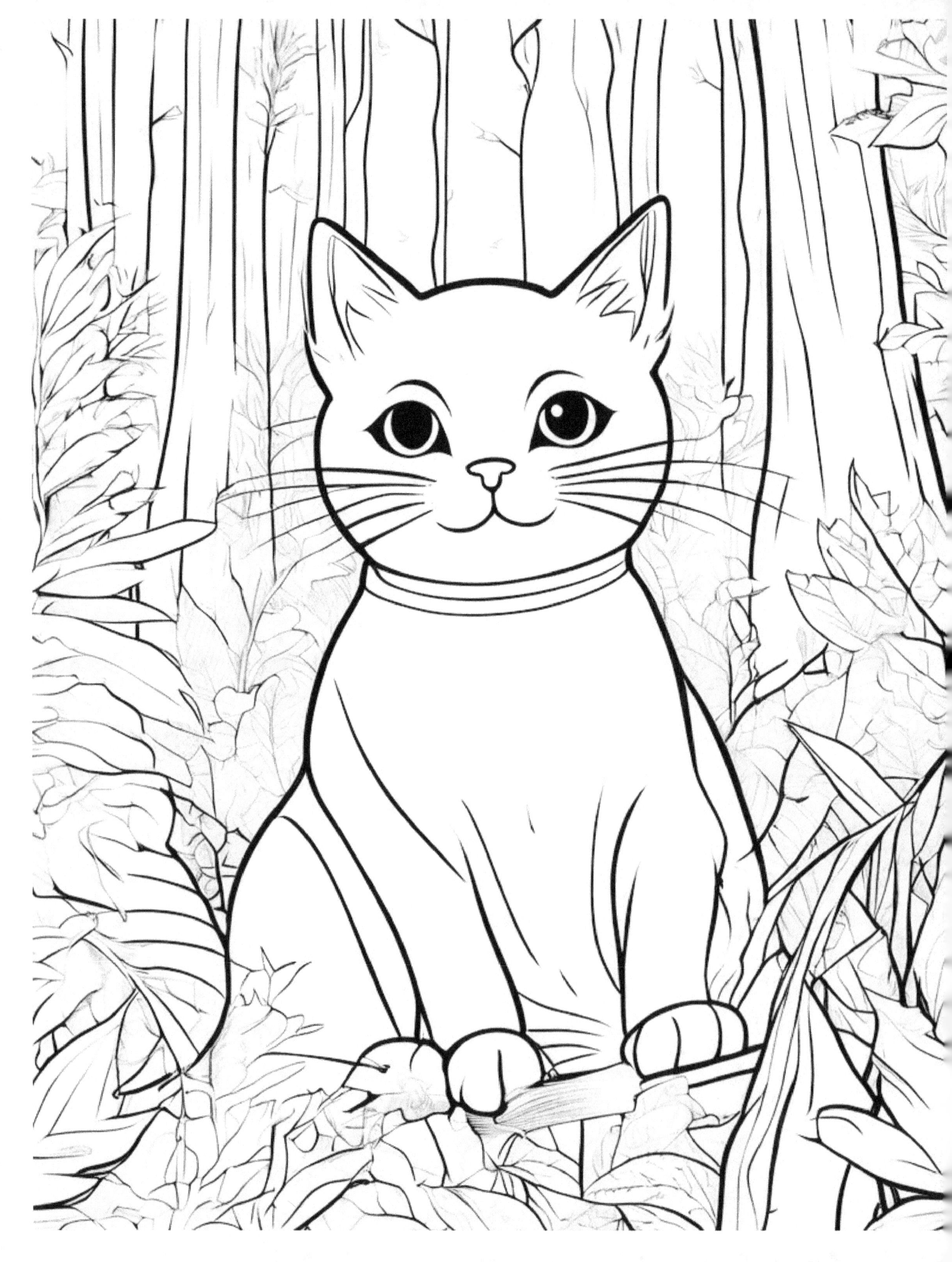

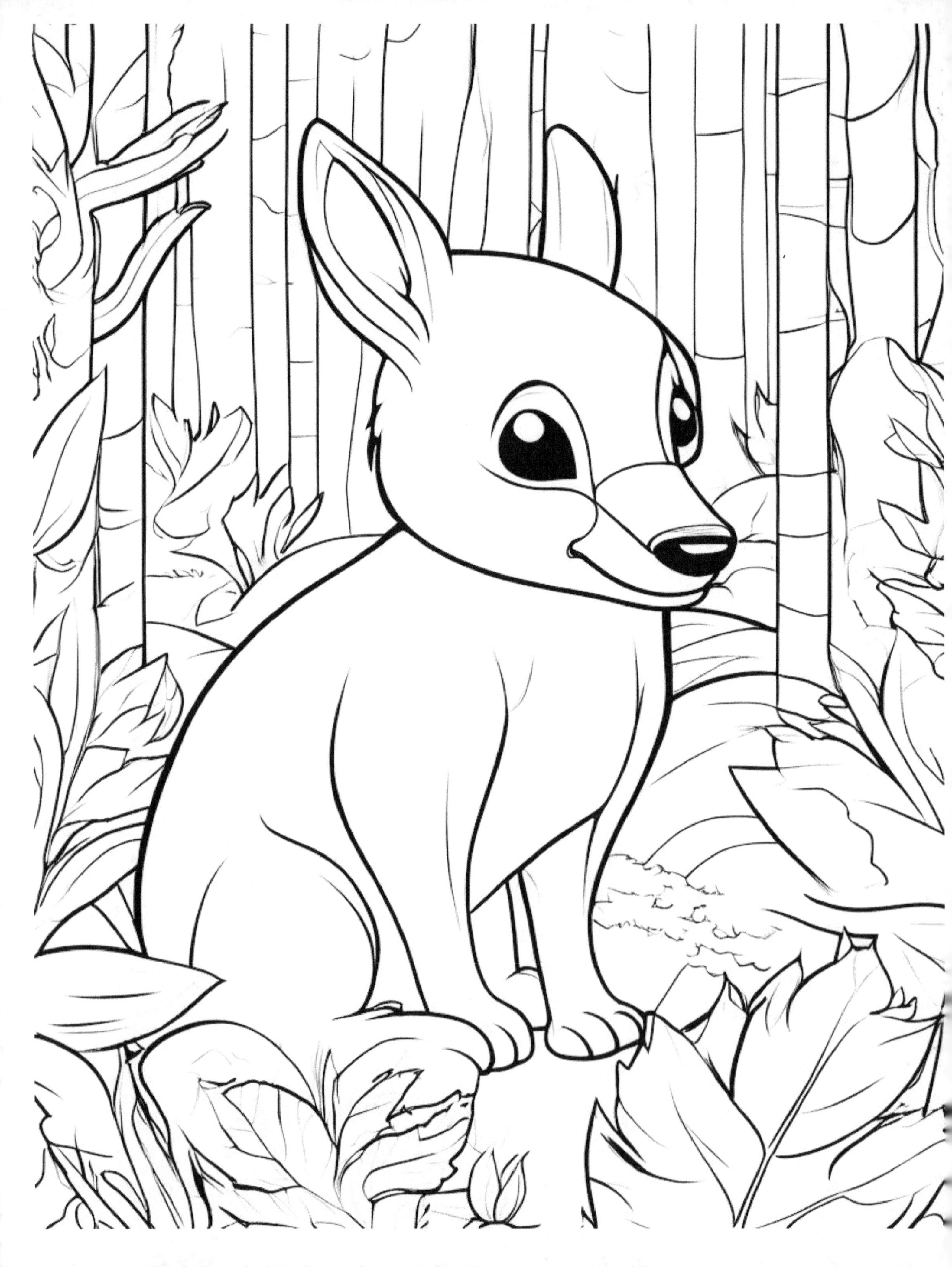

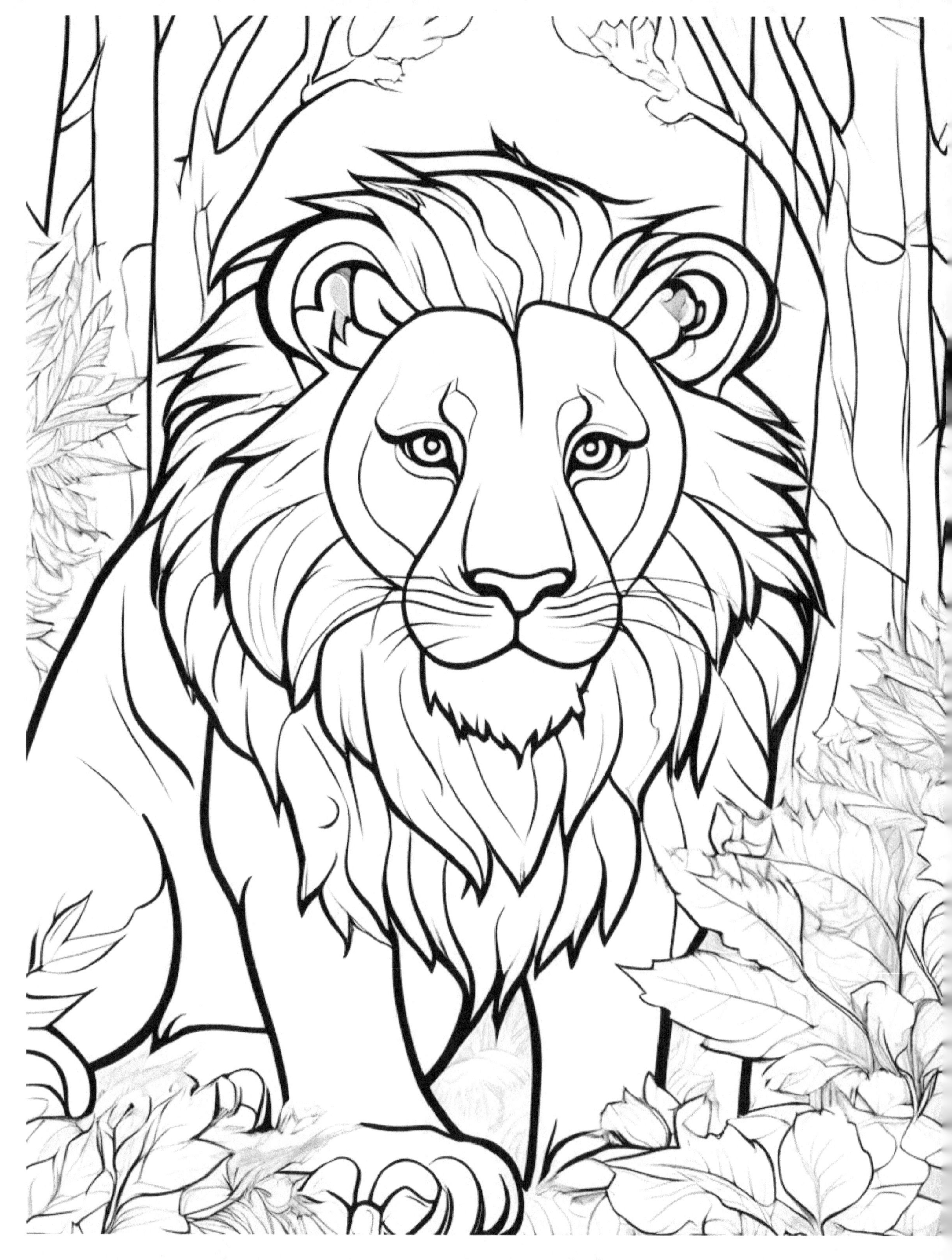

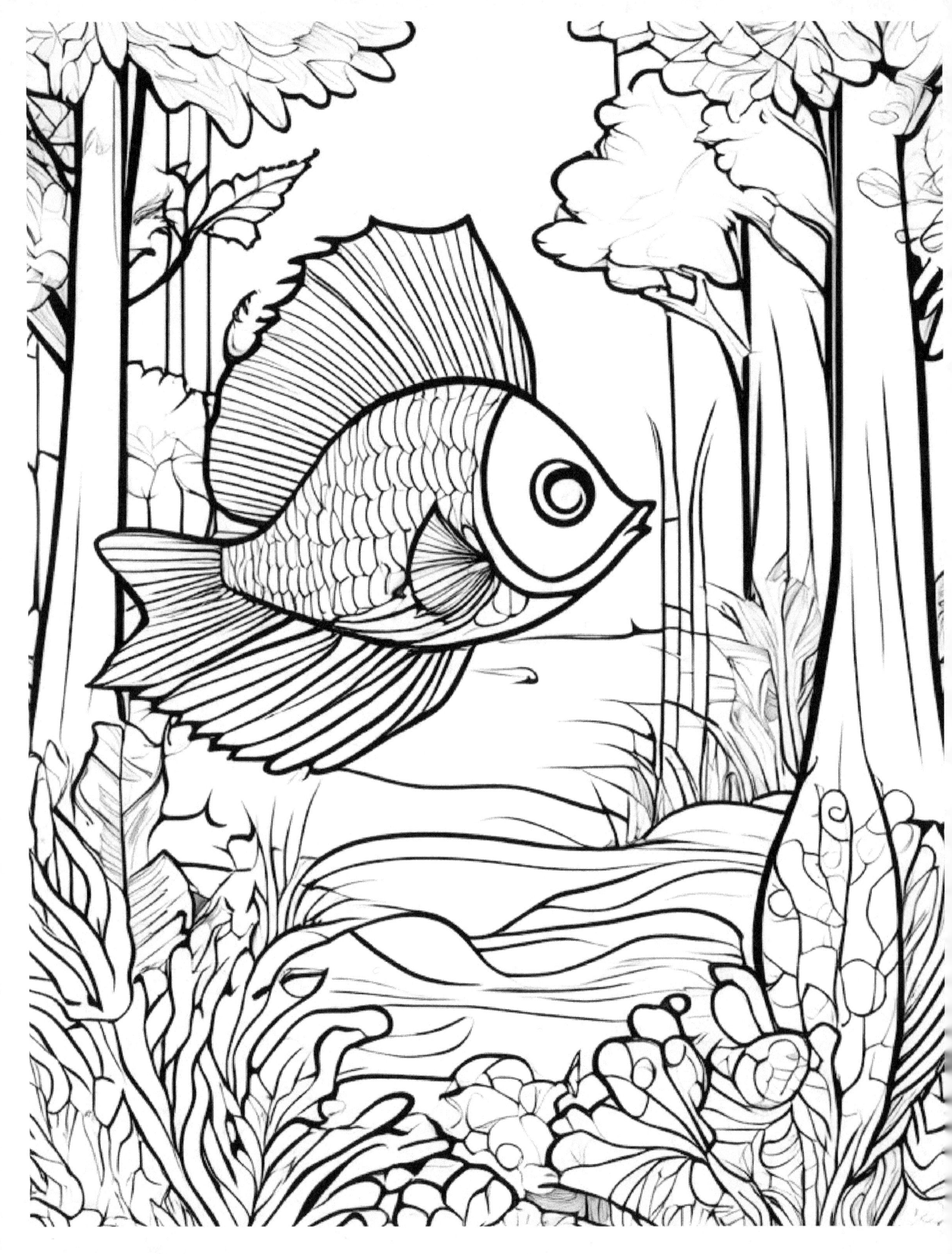